FATHERLESS REFLECTIONS on the FATHERHOOD of GOD

By David Kosobucki

Foreword by Mike MacIntosh

PathBinder
Publishing LLC
COLUMBUS, INDIANA

Published by PathBinder Publishing
P.O. Box 2611
Columbus, IN 47202
www.PathBinderPublishing.com

Edited by Brian Blair
Front cover photo illustration by Maddie Bellware
Back cover photo of author by Olivia Douglass
Covers designed by Paul J. Hoffman

First published in 2025
Manufactured in the United States

ISBN: 978-1-955088-90-9
Library of Congress Control Number: 2025901749

In Memory of All of My Parents

TESTIMONIALS

In *Fatherless Reflections on the Fatherhood of God*, David Koso-bucki strikes a chord that resonates throughout our modern culture. We are living in a global epidemic of failed families and forgotten fathers. Whether forgotten because they were never there or because they failed, the result has been a huge fracture in many societies. *Fatherless Reflections on the Fatherhood of God* paints a clear picture of the one faithful Heavenly Father over the dark canvas of earth's faithless fathers. It is a timely book with the only remedy for this disease – a Biblical understanding of our True Father.

– Jed Gourley, missionary pastor in the country of Georgia; author, *Distant Fields: The Amazing Call of George Markey from Farmland to Missions*

As an adoptive dad and YMCA chaplain, I can wholeheartedly attest to the fact that fatherlessness is a massive issue in our current culture. Having served alongside of Dave in ministry over the last several years, I am confident that his personal experience and his faith will significantly help those who struggle to see the relevance of the fatherhood of God in this generation.

– Josh Heaston, Director of Christian Mission, YMCA of Greater Indianapolis

This book is a must read! It is well written. Dave is real and transparent. It gives glory to God. I highly recommend it.

– Bill Goodrich, founding pastor, Horizon Christian Fellowship Indianapolis; Chairman Emeritus, Horizon University

What is a father? Perhaps like me, you had a father who was a role model of love and faithfulness. Unfortunately, such role models are not always the case. Drawing on his own childhood experience of fatherlessness, Dr. David Kosobucki reflects on the meaning of fatherhood and the character of God as our Heavenly Father. He writes with the kind of authenticity and vulnerability that comes only from a position of security. For David, that position is the assurance that comes from being a child of God. Reading David's book on fatherlessness was helpful for me in the recent loss of my earthly father, reassuring me that my Heavenly Father will never leave me nor forsake me.

– Randall Dodge, Ph.D., J.D.; President, Horizon University

This book is a wonderful message of hope, prayer, and love. David tells his life story and blends it so perfectly with an inspirational message of God being the most important Father in everyone's life. My growing up and not having the constant support and guidance of a father, this book opened my eyes to the grace and love that our heavenly Father provides to all.

– Mark Emmerson, David's half-brother, who, without being asked, pointed out several typos that all other early readers or editors missed. We are definitely related.

ACKNOWLEDGMENTS

The biggest thanks of all goes to Ginger for being married to me all these years. You and the kids really deserve more of an apology than a thank you, since the kind of person who could write this book presents a special challenge to his own family. So, thanks, or sorry, or whatever you deem most necessary from my side. I mean it. Ginger also was the first to read my work and make suggestions.

Thank you to the people, especially the leadership and board of Horizon Central CityWay Church in downtown Indianapolis for allowing me the kind of flexibility needed to work on a project like this. The same goes for Randall Dodge, PhD, and students, faculty and other administration of Horizon University. It is such a wonderful privilege to work with all of you. Still, you allowed me so much space that I managed somehow to get time away and make this book happen. Thank you, pastors Mike MacIntosh and Bill Goodrich, for going out in obedience and starting your churches, growing Horizon University, and allowing me a place to serve. Specific thanks to Angie Roberts for reading and suggesting numerous edits, almost all of which were incorporated into the final product.

Thank you, Julie Bouwens, for being among the first to read the early chapters and helping me go in the right direction. If my voice is not clear, it is my fault not yours. Thanks also to Noel Bouché, Luke Smith and Rob Bouwens and the guys of Canyon Pathways for early, unexpected and much-needed encouragement.

A super special thanks to Pastor Jed Gourley of Calvary Chapel in Tbilisi, Georgia (that's the country, not the state). I think you know that most of this book was written in your office when you were not there. The hospitable people of Calvary Tbilisi made me feel so right at home, it's almost embarrassing to describe.

Thanks to Joy McClain for connecting me with Paul Hoffman and PathBinder. And thanks to Paul Hoffman for being willing to publish the book. Thank you, Brian Blair, for being more of an encourager than an editor and helping me get this out.

A long-time pastor and provost of a Christian University might be expected to give thanks to God in whatever he does, and that seems on one level just a platitude or formula kind of thing. Yet, for those of us who in fact walk with Jesus, and understand that He is Lord, it's not cliché at all. We owe a greater debt to God our Father and Jesus our Savior than we will ever be able to pay back. Since we are saved by grace, paying it back never enters the question. We really are and shall be "giving thanks always and for everything to God the Father in the name of our Lord Jesus Christ." (Eph 5:20)

FOREWORD

"A good father is one of the most unsung, unpraised, unnoticed, and yet one of the most valuable assets in our society."
– Billy Graham

I was fatherless, as many are around the world today. Being fatherless lent to drugs, alcohol, bar room brawls, and many of the issues our doctors, psychologists, and psychiatrists deal with on a daily basis, not to mention the loss of work, breaking laws, and many of twenty-first century's social ills.

It was a big chip on my shoulder growing up, until I found out I was not without a father. After being divorced for three years, my wife and I remarried. We had two small children. The day of the wedding I prayed, "God, I don't know how to be a father." A still, small voice said, "I will be your role model."

I have known David for many decades. As his pastor and friend, I have known him to be a deep thinker. In this book, David hands us a key to happiness. He has discovered, like I did, that God loves His children and will never leave them nor forsake them.

To every heartbroken child, let this book heal your heart. Take your time reading, taking notes, and reflecting as you turn the pages.

Bravo, David. Well done!

– Mike MacIntosh
Founding pastor, Horizon Christian Fellowship, San Diego;
Founder and Chairman Emeritus, Horizon University

INTRODUCTION

*"And I will be father to you, and you shall be sons
and daughters to me, says the Lord Almighty"*
–2 Cor. 6.18

I agree with and understand why Billy Graham made that statement about fathers that my pastor, Mike, quotes at the beginning of
his foreword. Yet the concept of God's Fatherhood is not one that I
easily understand. When I say this, I mean it in a personal way. The
dictionary definition of a father is not that hard to grasp. The same
goes for the idea of fatherhood that we find in biology, as in being
the male parent and not the female one. Having grown up Catholic,
the words Father, Son, and Holy Spirit roll easily off my tongue.
This, however, is all a bit abstract or impersonal and, as I read the
Bible, it seems that God's Fatherhood ought to be more than an
abstraction. There should be childlike feelings of dependence and
a sense of attachment. There should be some naturally understood
love and loyalty mixed with a measure of respect. These are the
parts that do not come naturally to me. In this, I know that I am not
alone, and it may be due to an epidemic of fatherlessness.

There is a well-documented lack of fatherhood in the world
today, not least here in the USA. For better or worse, I am an
example of that trend. As a result, my reflections on fatherhood,
and even the Fatherhood of God, do not come from a place of rich
and wide experience. They mostly pour forth from a vacuum. The
big lessons about what it means to be a father or even to have one,

were never exactly offered and therefore never learned and, until much too recently, not consciously missed. There is more than one way to respond to this absence of understanding.

For many who share my experience, or have that same lack of experience, it seems that the preferred way to handle a father's absence is to conclude that fathers are non-essential. We are free, after all, to belittle the concept, blame the evil patriarchy for insisting upon their own necessity, and say that we are better off without them – or at least no worse off than we would be if they were around. In our present cultural moment, we are free to decide that fathers are optional. I would suggest that this course of action is a mistake.

To the extent that the role of the father is diminished, people might distance themselves from the Fatherhood of God that is seen in the pages of the Bible. This is unhelpful, and we can see where this first option is taking us. If we insist that we are right to not value fathers and fatherhood, then the Fatherhood of God becomes optional as well – perhaps even a lingering form of ancient oppression. This is what many have done, but there are consequences. For example, we can easily end up evaluating the Bible by our own opinions. If the Bible is the word of God as it claims to be, and as traditional Christians believe, then we are making a major break with history and with Scripture itself. In these pages, I intend to take a different course.

Instead of using our ignorance of fatherhood as the standard, what if we assume the Bible is correct? In that case, seeing God more clearly as our heavenly Father would open doors to understanding God in the way he has revealed himself in the Scriptures. It would allow us to see our Father much the way the Son evidently saw him and still sees him now. It would help us to relate to God in ways we never learned to relate to anyone, and in ways that Jesus himself not only knew and practiced, but highly valued. A close relationship with his Father came naturally to Jesus, just as it might seem unnatural to us. Many of us, and certainly I, need to make that fundamental change.

For example, I long to pray the prayer that begins, "Our Father" with a deeper awareness of what God's Fatherhood means, and that is only the beginning. I want there to be a closeness and a trust and a host of other things, most of which I cannot even name because I suspect I do not even know what they are. But I genuinely want to know and experience them, or better, I genuinely want to know him in the way that he wants to be known. One goal that I have in these reflections is to overcome the obstacle of fatherlessness so that I might better appreciate, know, and experience the Fatherhood of God. As we begin this journey, we will have a starting place. In other words, I am making some assumptions, at least three that I can name straight off.

The first assumption I am making is that God is bigger than my problem. Yes, I see fatherlessness as a problem, but it is not an insurmountable one. If God is a Father and God is still God, then there is no difficulty this fallen world can throw at him that will make him duck or cringe or run away as if he is defeated. If we have not come to appreciate human fatherhood on earth, let us begin with our Father in heaven. The same God who created everything out of nothing can give us a worthy idea of his Fatherhood where none has ever existed before. To the extent that there is something here to learn, I desire to learn it, and with God's help there will be lessons in the following reflections that will make a difference in my faith, my life, and my relationship with him.

My second assumption, as mentioned above, is that I do not believe I am alone. With fatherlessness being so widespread, there are likely others that find themselves in the same position. They may have similar experiences or may know many others who do. And they are not yet ready to throw fatherhood, especially God's Fatherhood, in the dumpster. These individuals may share similar questions. They may ask, "What does it even mean that God is my Father?" They may wonder whether or why it should be important to think of God in such terms. Connected with that, they wonder why Christ would reveal himself as the Son. Yet, there it is in the Bible, where all of us can see it, which brings us to another assumption I shall make.

Assumption three is that the Bible gives us the most accurate viewpoint we can find. If Christ instructed us to see God as our

Father, then that is precisely what we should do. The Bible is there to teach us as God's holy word. If something within it does not make enough sense to us, then that is only showing us an area in which we have room to grow. This is helpful for it gives us direction. The Holy Spirit has inspired the text of Scripture for this very purpose. Let us allow the Spirit to be our teacher and the Bible to be our text, so that we do not have to stay where we are, ignorant of something that might turn out to be of incredible worth.

Before we dig too far into Scripture to learn these lessons, allow me to relate something of my own experience of fatherlessness. I want to do this not because this experience is more real, more tragic, or more authoritative than anyone else's. Others may have more to say in this area than I do, and what they say may be more insightful. Still, since these are my own reflections, I believe I owe it to you, dear reader, to let you know a bit about myself.

It will provide context for the reflections that follow. It may help you understand why I say a certain thing or say it in a certain way. If I begin with a bit of my own story, it may help you read the personal reflections as coming from someone who is not a stranger. My hope is that some familiarity with my background will make the thoughts seem more real for being those of a person whose situation is not unfamiliar. We will soon be exploring views and concepts that are intended to draw us closer to the Father that I hope we already share as his adopted children. Our connection with the Father, through Jesus his Son, is a relationship that will last into eternity and which we can appreciate more even now. But first, let me give you my fatherless credentials.

Table of Contents

CHAPTER 1
FATHERLESSNESS – PART 1

"What happened if an unwanted child gave birth to an unwanted child? It was as though she were in a hall of mirrors, except that instead of getting smaller in each one she got younger and younger."
— Heather O'Neill, *The Lonely Hearts Hotel*

The story of my fatherlessness starts at least one generation earlier. My biological mother, Frances Kościołek, was not her father's daughter. Her mother, Aniela, was married to Józef Kościołek. She evidently had an affair, or something, with Bolesław Koszelak, who lived next door at the time. Frances was the result. Bolesław already had a wife and family in Poland and eventually brought them to *Ameryka* but was staying at this point with his brother-in-law Antoni. Some relatives and I figured this out with the help of some now-available documents and DNA testing. No one ever talked about it publicly, but privately, it is likely that a lot of people knew. How could you keep such things a secret in a tight-knit ethnic neighborhood back in the 1920s, where the forces at work were that of an urban small town?

In small towns, people know things and they talk about them. In the roaring Twenties, the same would have been true on the East Side of Buffalo, N.Y. Among those who probably had the strongest inkling of Frances's biological origins would have been Józef Kościołek, the husband of Aniela. It is hard to say what all this did to the family dynamics of their household or the emotional well-being of Frances, but I doubt if it was helpful. What was her relationship like with the man who helped raise her, whose surname she carried around throughout her life? Did he love her deeply as one of his own? Did he reject her outright, or was it somewhere in the middle? Did the lack of father-child resemblance nag at his heart daily even though he tried his best to be a father to the child of his wife and his next-door neighbor? Did Frances have any relationship at all with her biological father Bolesław, whose family, it seems, tried to keep the fact that Frances was such a close relative cloaked in silence? The possibility that she felt rejected by both of her fathers, not to mention at least some half-siblings, is very real.

David Kosobucki's birth mother, Frances Kościołek, in June 1959. David was born that September.

What did the neighbors think, know, or say about this arrangement, and what impact did that have on Frances while growing up? How about kids in the neighborhood or at school, knowing that children can be cruel to those who are different or have an unusual story behind them? What would have gone through Frances's mind if she saw a child bringing her hand up alongside her mouth and whispering a secret in another child's ear, perhaps timidly glancing in Frances's direction?

In what ways did any or all of this factor into Frances's future and future relationships? She never graduated from high school and later entered into an unwise, short-lived marriage. How exactly did that happen? What were the detailed twists and turns that carried her along the path that her life eventually followed? And what stories

The author's original birth certificate, issued by the New York State Department of Health. Note that no information regarding a father is included.

lie in the origins of the three children born to her after that marriage was over, each with a different father, none of whom she ever married? I am the third of those children and the only one her half-sister Janina, or Jane, ever knew about. Her first two children, Suzanne and Mark, were born during a period of several years that Frances was separated from her family. My Aunt Jane told me of this time of separation, and that Frances returned home pregnant with me. Suzanne, Mark, and I are now all in contact with each other.

During that period of separation, Frances never wandered far from Buffalo. All three of us children were born there, in the now nonexistent Deaconess Hospital. Arriving one year after the next, we went directly into unrelated foster homes and were all later adopted by those families. Our original birth certificates each have only a blank space where the name of the father is supposed to be. What more perfect way can there be to document the fatherlessness that so many people experience?

As indicated above, it is likely that my biological mother Frances felt some measure of rejection from her own biological relatives, especially on her father's side. She probably did not perfectly fit in growing up in her mother's home either, knowing that her father was not her father, so to speak, and her brother and sister were biological half-siblings. It seems as if her sister Jane and brother Alfred completely accepted Frances. Jane, who is the only one of the three siblings my family and I ever met, seemed to love Frances as any sister would and spoke of her in affectionate, respectful tones. All the written communication we have from Alfred, acquired from Jane's estate after she died, indicates a closeness between him and his sisters and all of them with their mother. At any rate, there is nothing that would indicate that Frances was kicked out of the house or even felt unwelcome after a certain age. And yet, she went missing for several years.

There is likely an inner explanation for the long stretch without contact with her family and it all fits together with some already mentioned aspects of her life. Frances did not finish school, though Jane and Alfred did. Neither Jane nor Alfred ever married or had any children, though Alfred's short life explains why in his case. Alfred died in WWII when his plane went down off the coast of North Africa. No one on board survived. Frances married once, ill-advisedly. According to Jane, he was not a good husband, though we have no details as to why not. Nonetheless, the marriage did not last long. Frances then had three children, all outside the context of marriage. These are signs of inner conflict in Frances.

Sometimes acts that might look like rebellion are the outworking of an inner turmoil. Speaking as one who knows a bit of this from experience, it does not take a full-blown rejection to make a person of questionable birth feel like they do not precisely belong. For some people in this category, a natural sense of disconnection, where others seem naturally at ease, is their usual frame of reference. Home, for example, is not a place where they feel *at home*. Such a person can then go searching for the place and the people among which they belong. This was, I believe, the case with Frances. It is not hard to fill in the gaps, even if we do so imprecisely.

She married unwisely, perhaps hastily, as a way of feeling like she belonged somewhere and to someone, but that soon ended in divorce. Her brother and stepfather had already both died, so when she began to wander, it was her mother and sister she left behind. This is when she began to have children.

When a woman gives birth to three babies, all with different fathers, year after year, and gives them all away at birth, there must be an explanation, but none of the options speak of an easy life. Was there perhaps some actual defiance? The desire to make one's own way in the world is strong for some people, and a streak of independence may have played into Frances's departure. Still, defiance alone would leave our explanation terribly shallow.

To what extent was Frances reacting to a sense of shame? Her origins were always something she was probably forced to hide and felt ashamed of when other people knew. Being forced to tell lies and keep secrets about yourself from childhood will inevitably take an emotional toll. A failed marriage in an environment where divorce was both uncommon and frowned upon only added to Frances's disgrace. That longing to fit in, to forever belong some-where and with someone would, at this stage, only have grown and probably to an unhealthy degree. A person like this is already near to being a victim and is almost waiting for an assailant.

The list of unscrupulous suitors may have been long, and it is possible that not all of them were unscrupulous, they were simply unattached. This was in the post-war, baby-boom era of the 1950s, when people were falling in love and getting married all the time. We can envision it starting when one available man or another persuaded Frances to go off with him. There may have been prom-ises made or implied and, longing for acceptance, Frances went along. A few years and a few men later, she returned to her mother and sister, now pregnant with me.

My family and I received a good deal of written communi-cation, saved by Jane, after she passed away in 2014. Some of it from her brother Alfred, when he was in the military and some of it is between the families of the men who died with him when their plane went down. Other letters are in Polish from the time period when the failing communist government imposed martial law. We believe Frances was the one who saved all of this and probably wrote the letters to Poland, since this collection was kept in her room. In all of it together, whether from Alfred, Jane or Frances, there is little to say about their father. That brings us to the part of the story where Frances's fatherlessness leads to me.

CHAPTER 2
FATHERLESSNESS – PART 2

"Memory, I realize, can be an unreliable thing; often it is heavily co-loured by the circumstances in which one remembers, and no doubt this applies to certain of the recollections I have gathered here."
– Kazuo Ishiguro, *A Pale View of Hills*

So far, I have told a little of the story of Frances Kościołek, and that is really about all of it that I know. Even some of that is what I would call *educated conjecture*. So again, when Frances returned home to Jane and their mother, she was pregnant with me. I have a photo dated June 1959, which would have been about the time of their little family reunion. I am in it, inside that slightly bulging tummy.

At the time I met my Aunt Jane, I knew there were two chil-dren born before me, thanks to non-identifying information given to me by the State of New York. I asked her about them, think-ing that maybe she knew more than I did. I only knew that such children existed – no name, age, whether boy or girl, alive or not – nothing else, just two births prior to me. At that point, the con-versation became awkward. Poor old Aunt Jane had no idea what I was talking about. At age 89, she not only met me and my family, but heard that Frances had two more children. She may not have even believed me and only lived a few months longer, so I have no way to know how that relationship or further conversations about

Frances might have progressed. In any event, Jane did not know that there were two earlier children, who I now know to be my half siblings, Suzanne and Mark.

A few months after the above-mentioned photo, in September of 1959, Frances went to Deaconess Hospital in Buffalo to give birth for the third time in three years. When Frances left the hospital, she left without me. I was taken home from the hospital by Casimir and Florence Kosobucki who paid the medical expenses for Frances in exchange for her newborn child. The transaction was arranged by Dr. Adolph Smith, MD, who was the family doctor for both Florence and Frances, a detail which was confirmed by Jane. In our day this sounds a bit shady, like a gray market baby sale, but at the time I do not believe it was all that strange. The foster care system was not as highly developed as it is now. Presumably, the conversation went something like, "I know a woman who is soon to give birth to a child but does not intend to keep it. Would you like it?" Not being able to have children of their own, Mr. and Mrs. Kosobucki agreed. Shortly after I was circumcised, as Florence described it, I went with them to my first-ever home.

My legal name, if we can truly call it that, was Male Kosciolek, the unnamed male child of Frances and a blank line. A year later, I was officially adopted by the Kosobuckis and legally switched identities from simply Kosciolek, as it says on my *original* birth certificate, or Male Kosciolek, as it says on my adoption certificate, to David Casimir Kosobucki, which is what it says on my *legal* birth certificate. For those unfamiliar with this practice, many states, like New York, issue a new birth certificate when a child is adopted, which names the adoptive parents as if they are the only parents the child has ever had. This becomes the legal birth certificate. Supposedly the practice started to keep a person from being embarrassed when, as in the case of all three of Frances Kosciolek's children, there is no father named. That makes a degree of sense, since the adoptee can, when needed, legally present a birth certificate that looks more normal, with two parents and no mention of adoption. Why draw attention to that inelegant story when at times all that counts is where and when you were born? The practical purpose of the policy decreases vastly when the original birth certificate is declared legally off limits even to you, the child, even when you are an adult with children of your own, and even when your birth mother is dead. That is how it was for the better part of a century in New York until it changed in January 2020. But none of that mattered to me as a baby in 1959.

An Adopted Child

At this point, I need to be delicate in anything I say so as not to misrepresent the real-life experience of life in my adopted home. The problem arises out of the fact that all adoptees and adoptive parents are imperfect people in an imperfect world. The Bible gives the most satisfactory explanation for that which

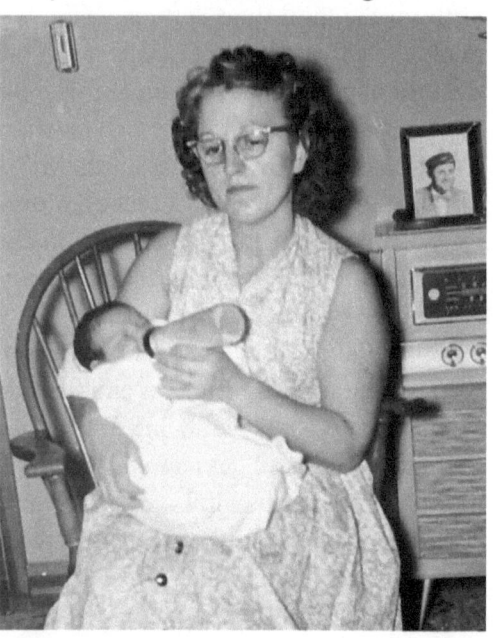

David Kosobucki's adoptive mother, Florence Kosobucki, feeding him in October 1959. A photo of his adoptive father, Casmir Kosobucki, is in the background.

I have ever encountered by saying that God created everything good, even very good, but that these things were corrupted by humanity's fall into sin. The relevant result of that profound doctrine is that I was an imperfect child adopted by an imperfect couple. My childhood environment was not horrible, but neither was it ideal. It was difficult, as sometimes adoptive homes can be for both the children and their parents, but I am not laying the blame upon anyone. Non-adoptive families can have issues too.

Florence, my adopted mother, was extremely limited in her cognitive abilities, while being constantly driven by her emotions, impressions, and fear of the unknown. I was the opposite, having better-than- average mental capacity, lower- than-average emotional range, and a natural bent to explore the unfamiliar. The result of this disparity, which I chalk up to the simple genetics of our particular adoptive household, was usually frustration. Often, when I learned something new from school or a friend, I would assume all adults had adequate ability to grasp the information and a comparable appetite to learn. I would try to get my mom to understand this thing that was beyond her capabilities. She would be absorbed in feelings and fears that I could never feel, nor even imagine as a teenage boy possessing all (or likely even less of) the emotional maturity normally inherent in that phase of life. This was not fun for either of us, and I would not wish the challenge on anyone else.

A perfect example of this disparity is what my wife, Ginger, has dubbed my *Copernicus moment*. One day at school, when I was in the second grade, we learned all about the planets and how they revolved around the sun. I found this fascinating. Moreover, every Polish person needs to know this, since Copernicus, or Mikołaj Kopernik as he is known in some circles, was the first to document this *revolutionary* idea, and Copernicus was a Pole. (Galileo evidently got the whole idea from him.) Being Polish both genetically and by adoption, I diligently absorbed the lesson. And then I came home.

Did I say *every* Polish person needs to know this? Well, one did not, and that was my mother. What might have been a cheerful, "What did you learn in school today?" conversation, turned into an argument. My mother would simply not believe me when I told her that the planets revolved around the sun. In fact, we could not even talk about the planets. We got stuck at the point where the sun had to revolve around the earth because it was obviously true. At age seven, I was now starting to grasp, "She does not know this, does not believe me, and is convinced that I am wrong. She believes the teacher somehow misled me, or perhaps that I misunderstood the lesson." It turns out that the Copernicus moment was only the beginning.

Allegedly Mark Twain said something like, "When I was eighteen, my old man was stupid. By the time I was twenty-five, I could not believe how much he had learned in the preceding seven years." We all get the joke because all kids think their parents lack smarts and then the kids grow up and begin to know better. In my case, that was true in the area of maturity, I suppose, but as far as my mother was concerned, there were only rare moments when she turned out to know something that I did not. I say "rare moments" to allow for any biased, selective memory on my part, but in fact I cannot think of any. My mother was really that severely limited in her abilities. She went to school for a year or two beginning at age 7 or 8 and then stopped, never to return. She never learned to read beyond a kindergarten level. Cognitively, she seemed to stop growing right around the point where a child would be in second grade. Her social skills were better than that, which made it possible for her to fool a lot of people. But again, as far as intelligence, we would classify her as *special needs,* or *special ed,* or whatever the current term is today.

When I have told this story in the past, one of the most common responses is that the listener does not believe it is true. Admittedly, it sounds like an unlikely life. Another response is to wonder how the adoption was allowed to go forward. This, I think, is applying the standards for adoptive parents used in the twenty-first century to evaluate the situation of a child born in 1959. Things were different then and marketable babies were something of a commodity.

Finally, I have often been asked if maybe my mom was dyslexic and how that may have contributed to her lack of reading skills. Maybe she was dyslexic. I am no expert in learning difficulties. What I do know is that she could hardly understand anything that I felt was important, and this kept the level of tension high in our home. I was a kid, not a trained social worker or special education teacher. Since for much of my early life it was just the two of us, though she loved me, the relationship was strained.

I want to emphasize that she loved me, which is important in an adoptive relationship. She did what she could to provide for our needs and we got help from other people. If there was any lack of love, it was undoubtedly from me toward her. Yet even what love there was had an exceedingly difficult aspect to it. Since my mother was so limited in her abilities, her love for me was something like the love that a little girl has for her dolly. This is normal and endearing in little girls, but in normal life it is the little girl that then grows up. The baby doll stays the same and ends up somewhere in the attic or on a shelf as the girl gets older. In our case, it was the baby doll that grew up. The little girl did not know how to handle it and neither did the dolly. Suffice it to say that she had to depend on other people for a lot of things, and a certain percentage of that dependence fell upon me.

Thankfully, when in her seventies, Florence came to a personal faith in Christ. I had the privilege of taking part in her baptism. She then lived to be ninety-four, so I had ample opportunity to see that her faith was real. Her generosity was unsurpassed and her ability to show kindness to just about anyone left a mark on more people than I will ever know. Our relationship grew marginally better, but with all the baggage that had built up in the preceding decades, it still left something to be desired. I look forward to spending eternity together, knowing that it will be a time when we will be able to relate to one another without sin or any of its effects, with perfected minds and bodies and with all the difficulties forever gone. My father, on the other hand, passed away before either my mother or I came to Christ.

Fatherless a Second Time

Casimir, or Casey as everyone called him, died when I was thirteen and he was forty-seven, leaving me the only adopted child of a widowed mom. As far as I can remember, I never had much in common with my adopted dad, Casey Kosobucki. This was probably disappointing to him, though I had no ability to imagine that as a child. Every father wants a son that can be a chip off the old block, and I know I was nothing like that to him as a young boy. I cannot say I ever thought about it as a child, but as an adult, I have sometimes wished we had more time together. It would have been possible to get to know him better than my thirteen-year-old self was able to manage before he died. Maybe we had more in common than our shared ability to be emotionally distant and frequently irritated. Are those characteristics a product of nature or nurture? I am not sure. This is partly because I know even less about the father I had before him, not even a name.

To this day, I still wonder about my biological father whose name I have never known, the man whose name might have appeared in the blank space in my original birth certificate. What was he like? What was his name anyway, and what would it have been like to go through life knowing it, sharing a surname, and having documents that expressed the source of my Y chromosome and fully half of my DNA? Nurture might be out of the question, but what natural similarities do I have to him that I may never know? And why wasn't his name recorded? Is it possible that Frances did not even know? The fact that there are three children, all biological half-siblings who share her as a mother, indicates that there may have been some question as to who our fathers were, rather than just a reluctance to name them in our legal documents.

To divulge a little of my inner dreamworld, I have sometimes imagined that my biological father was someone famous, which I understand is not an unusual fantasy for adopted children. If he was famous and word somehow got out that he was my father, it might be something of a scandal. But then it would only be a scandal for him, not for me, because I would enjoy having a famous dad. From my side, I am either the spurious offspring (to use a polite term) of someone famous or the spurious offspring of someone ordinary, which I suppose is the most likely option.

Another unlikely possibility, but one that fuels my imagination is that my father was someone notoriously bad – like an infamous Nazi collaborator who left Poland posing as a refugee. (My lack of Germanic DNA makes an authentic Nazi less likely.) Or maybe a serial criminal from whom my mother escaped. Or someone with more spurious offspring than he could even count and just as many neglected, abandoned mothers. (Though if that were true, we might have found each other through DNA testing by now.) Having a famous (or even infamous) biological dad seems to me like a good option, though less likely than that he was just an ordinary guy. It is very possible that he never even knew about me, because unlike mothers and motherhood, fathers are not automatically aware they have fathered a child.

This last fact makes fatherhood in the deepest and most profound sense almost optional. A father can be a father on a more superficial and purely genetic level such as a sperm donor whose child is brought up in a distant home. And yet the more I think about it, the more I wonder which sense of fatherhood is deeper, the genetic father or the father who raised the child? They are both deep and important in their own way.

The biological side contributes much to the whole picture of who we are, and sometimes in surprising ways. There is the whole business of inherited traits and medical issues. There are those things people always say about kids, like they have their father's nose, or ears, or hair, not to mention the whole array of natural tendencies, abilities, or the lack thereof. Not knowing who the man is leaves a gap in one's self-understanding. That gap, while inevitable to some degree, might be less profound if an adopted father stepped in and raised a child into adulthood. Alas, the only father I ever knew died too young to make that happen. And it left me and my mom in the unenviable position of comprising a two-person household in which, at age thirteen, I was by far the more educated of the two. Less mature, but more educated. We needed a lot of help, and we got a lot, to be sure, but there is only so much a neighbor or relative can do. They cannot step in and completely fill the role of a father.

Fatherless Effects

As a fatherless adoptee, my longing to be like a father is very deep. So deep and so hidden, even to me, that for most of my life

I did not even know the desire was there. I shrugged the whole father thing off as something that did not matter. The older I got, however, the more I began to feel the need, though it was a need and a feeling that I could never actually name. Admitting the truth that I have lacked a man in my life to look up to as father has softened a nagging stress that I never fully felt until it was gone. Inner turbulence over this and related issues was as natural to my make up as the bitterness in black coffee. And just as with coffee, I was so accustomed to the acquired taste that I did not really taste it anymore. I needed a father but refused to admit it even to myself. The bitterness and the stress of that state remained, though I ignored it unconsciously and insistently.

As a result of my own experience, it is no surprise to me that so many men in prison have no connection to their fathers. I have also heard that fatherlessness has an impact on women, too. While different from the effect on men, it is often quite profound. From the male side, however, not knowing whom to be like, whom to emulate, whom to imitate, whom to follow, is a problem. Still, if you have this problem, it is the easiest thing in the world not to see it. You learn to figure things out, or at least that is what you tell yourself. You learn to be determined and that helps, to a certain extent, especially if you are determined to do positive, helpful things – to accomplish admirable goals. Unfortunately, you also learn to be selfish, not in the way a coddled or overprotected child is selfish, but selfish more in the way of a wolf or a rodent. It is selfishness with an aim to survive because survival may not feel like a fixed outcome in a cruel and unprotective world.

In a failed effort to be tough and to never be dominated by others, many young men overcompensate and turn to crime or other destructive behaviors. Therefore, we have that statistic of fatherless men being overrepresented in prisons. Sometimes it is very intentional. Just as often, I am convinced, it is the spontaneous reaction of the rodent brain which reflexively decides that fight or flight, or both together, is necessary under the circumstances. Those circumstances may or may not justify the response, but the response is still automatically there. We feel the need to fight when there is no enemy, but only an enemy perceived by the rodent-level brain. The response is not a dishonest pretense. It comes on because that is how the world really looks in the worldview of the fatherless boy. And it persists even when he is old enough that those unfamiliar with his plight think he should know better. Maybe he should, but he does not. His worldview needs corrective lenses, but no optometrist has ever shown him a clearer vision of life. Where can he turn?

Happily, I came to a personal faith in Christ when I was sixteen, three years after my father died. This prevented what might have been a worst-case scenario. For example, I never went to prison. And the fact that I came to Christ has given me the motivation to view God as my Father. I say "motivation," intentionally, rather than ability. Admittedly, knowing God as a Father is not a strong area, but it is an area in which I desire to grow. I also believe that I have walked with Jesus long enough that I can approach this subject with a level of maturity that I could not have had at an earlier period in my life. Before we move into the area of reflections, it might be helpful to review the assumptions that I first stated back in the Introduction. These assumptions will underlie all that follows throughout the rest of these pages.

My first assumption is that God is bigger than my *fatherlessness* problem and yours if that happens to be a problem we share. That brings us to the second assumption, which is that I do not believe I am alone. These days, there is more than enough of father absence to go around. Assumption three is that the Bible is right. In other words, if our questions need answers and our problems need solutions, the Bible is a good place to begin our search. For example, if we need a father, then the Father that we find in the pages of Scripture is precisely the Father that we need. We shall assume that the Bible portrays him as he truly is, not exhaustively perhaps, but to an extent that is sufficient for our requirements. Let us now begin with the first of our reflections, in which we will think about fatherhood, love and likeness.

CHAPTER 3
FATHERHOOD, LOVE, AND LIKENESS

"A man knows when he is growing old because
he begins to look like his father."
– Gabriel Garcia Marquez, *Love in the Time of Cholera*

I hope you now understand why I personally long to know God better as my Father. Deep down, I hope you long for the same thing. The details in the previous pages set us up for further reflection, and an opportunity to move on to some Scripture passages that relate to the Fatherhood of God. An instructive passage stands out in the First Letter of John:

> See what kind of love the Father has given to us, that we should be called children of God; and so we are. The reason why the world does not know us is that it did not know him. Beloved, we are God's children now, and what we will be has not yet appeared; but we know that when he appears we shall be like him, because we shall see him as he is. And everyone who thus hopes in him purifies himself as he is pure. (1 John 3:1-3)[1]

---

1 Unless otherwise noted, all biblical passages are from *The Holy Bible: English Standard Version* (Wheaton, Crossway Bibles, 2001).

God's Love

God has made us his children by choice because he loves us. In the natural world, children and parents pretty much get what they get, like it or not. Usually, I suppose it works out fairly well – not always perhaps, but more often than not. A family likeness can make understanding one another easier than in those cases where that likeness is not there. We sometimes hear, "The apple doesn't fall far from the tree," though I certainly do not remember ever hearing that kind of thing said about me growing up. The normally expected likeness was not fully present in the family of my mother, Frances, and it was not present for me.

The usual practice in those days was never to refer to either illegitimacy or adoption, so a child was simply expected to fit in. That was troubling because it never quite happened. If Hans Christian Andersen had not already written *The Ugly Duckling* story, I might have been motivated to write it myself. At present, though, many people share this trait of family non-resemblance in a world where traditional family structures have mostly dissolved, fathers are absent, and marriage has become harder to define. A thoroughly loving family can compensate agreeably for differences in DNA, but the love of that family is still vastly different and deficient when compared to the perfect love of God.

God's love for us, the kind of love that would make us his children, is like no other love. In adopting us into his family, he was fulfilling no needs of his own. The eternal and life-giving love present among the Persons of the Trinity was always perfect and complete. There was no need for God to create us. Christ lacked nothing that would have compelled him to redeem us. No requirement existed in the nature of the Holy Spirit that would prompt him to regenerate us so that we might enter this already perfect and perfectly loving Triune community. God never lacked for anyone to help with chores, run errands, assist him in the family business or take care of him in his old age.

There was love among the divine Persons, eternally existent and thoroughly satisfying, when we came along, and that love was extended to us. Our rebellion, both as a race and individually, did not repel the divine affection. It did nothing but push that love into self-sacrificing action on our behalf. This is what lies behind John's exclamation, "See what kind of love the Father has given to us ... (!)"

When we bring children into the world and they rebel, that is disappointing. Parents generally feel helpless in such situations and human love can then be tested to its limits. When you adopt proven and persistent rebels as your children, rebels who have already revolted against you personally, that is something else altogether. Infinite, uncompromising and insistent on completing its work to the very end, holy love was not induced by any felt need for self-fulfillment, the establishing of a legacy, or the cuteness of the child being adopted. Our very lack of a family resemblance, that lack of holiness and the presence of sin leading unto death, prompted the Holy One to fix what was wrong with us and make each one of his own. By faith, we are now children of God, and the family resemblance is growing all the time. That growing resemblance makes us unrecognizable to the world.

The Reason Why the World Does Not Know Us

Once we are children of God and the family resemblance to our Father begins increasing, we begin looking different from the world. As a result, the world does not know us. We no longer bear the resemblance to the world that the world hopes to see. Instead, we look like a Father, and a divine Brother, that the world does not know and has, in fact, rejected. The world cannot know us, at least not deep down, because it did not know Jesus. Consider the opening chapter of the Gospel of John:

> He was in the world, and the world was made through him, yet the world did not know him. He came to his own, and his own people did not receive him. But to all who did receive him, who believed in his name, he gave the right to become children of God, who were born, not of blood nor of the will of the flesh nor of the will of man, but of God. (John 1:10-13)

Family Likeness, or the Lack Thereof

It must have been terribly frustrating at times to have been born into ancient Israel and yet not be known or received by your own people. This was, after all, the one and only society on earth with immediate access to God, his words, and his works. And Jesus was, as the Nicene Creed would put it, "true God from true God, begotten, not made, consubstantial with the Father; through him all things were made." You might have thought that this nation would be the perfect place for God the Son to be born and accepted, but that was not the case.

As I have talked about earlier, my mother Frances probably did not quite fit in with her family and likely felt rejected from her biological father's side, if not by the father and family that she knew. I know something about not fitting in myself and many of us can relate to this at some level, but Christ is the ultimate example of not quite fitting in or being rejected.

For example, the difference between my adoptive mother and me was greater than most differences in other families that I have had the opportunity to see. Still, that difference was small compared to the difference between Christ and every last one of the people around him. He was of a different world and a different level of being. He was their creator and understood their thoughts and inner inclinations. This is apparent at times in the Gospels, though it is not easy to say how often Christ experienced such signs of omniscience. We can also be sure he was always correct in his opinions and when he knew something, he knew it with compete accuracy. In the Gospels we see that this sometimes led to arguments with his enemies, but the sinless Savior somehow kept his anger under control. (Whereas I, for example, did not, despite my not being omniscient.)

Not only did Christ control his anger so as never to cross the line into sin, but he also never even let this frustrating state of things hinder him along his pathway to the cross. His mission was to die for the people who were causing his frustration and he let nothing get in the way of that mission's fulfillment. Through this ultimate self-sacrifice, God welcomes us into the family life of the Trinity and our true home. We can receive him, believe in his name, and find ourselves to be children of God. Remarkable.

So, at present we differ from the world because we are no longer truly part of it as we once were. Yet the gap between us and God is in some ways still enormous, even though that very gap is what Christ bridged for us at the cross. Crossing that bridge from unholiness to holiness is no small thing. We may cross it positionally, but not cross it emotionally, cognitively, or behaviorally for quite some time. I am reminded of bridges that were part of my early life.

Mind the Gap

Growing up in Buffalo, on the border with Canada, meant that the option of international travel was always possible just by crossing one of the bridges over the Niagara River. Crossing the border by crossing the bridge was a normal thing to do, but my Canadian experience only went so far, in that I only ever crossed *positionally.* By paying a toll, passing the flags in the middle of the river, and answering a few questions for the customs officials, my friends and I got into Canada. We were there; we were in a different country, but that alone never made us Canadian. We may have enjoyed the colorful currency, but there was always the inner knowledge that it was not our own. The Queen Elizabeth Way (QEW) would take us through St. Catherines and Hamilton to Toronto, which was 100 miles or 161 km away, depending on your preference, but any special affection for the queen herself, her relatives, or all that was royal was not easy for us native New York Staters to rally. This majestic, regal lady was relegated by name, in my mind, mainly to the name of the highway and her noble face to Canadian coins.

All of this to say that our Christianity involves a similar gap and, if we *mind the gap* (hats off to the Toronto subway), it reveals to us where we need to grow. We may cross the bridge into the realm of holiness and sainthood positionally. Through Christ we enter God's family and are now *in Christ* officially, sharing a

Father that is still somehow uniquely his. And we can do this long before the other aspects of our nature and the desires of our hearts begin to catch up. We can be in the kingdom in one sense without sincere devotion to the King.

This is where going to Canada or any other county is so much different from entering God's kingdom. We might go to Canada as often as we like without our hearts becoming any more Canadian. Not so with the kingdom of God. As we cross over into God's kingdom, our hearts, minds, affections, and behavior will in fact change. They must, eventually. It may take what seems like too long and it will take some effort, but change shall most certainly come. We have to remember 1 John 3:2, "Beloved, we are God's children now, and what we will be has not yet appeared; but we know that when he appears we shall be like him, because we shall see him as he is." Change is coming whether we like it or not.

But we really should like that change. We should long for it. Greater transformation toward Christlikeness should be a priority, a preoccupation, an intense internal desire. The fact that "what we shall be has not yet appeared" reminds us that we are far enough from God's character and likeness that we really cannot fully grasp what godliness ought to be like. We were created in his image, yes, and we would reflect that image better, except that the fall has distorted the mirror's glass just enough that the reflection is not perfectly visible. As Paul reflects (pun intended) in 1 Cor 13:12, "For now we see in a mirror dimly, but then face to face. Now I know in part; then I shall know fully, even as I have been fully known." We see God's image imperfectly now, though we long for something better, which we cannot yet see. And it is okay, for now, if the "something better" is still not visible. One day we shall be like him.

The Father and Son (Dis)Connection

Earlier I mentioned my lack of obvious similarity or connection with my adopted father, Casey Kosobucki. Perhaps when I was young, some similarity would have drawn us together, rather than the differences keeping us apart. My entire lack of knowledge of my other father, the one who gave me his DNA, creates an even larger measure of self-consciousness, since I do not even know who he is. In both cases, the father-child relationship is not pleasingly comfortable.

Our relationship to God as our Father is not and never will be like the father-child relationships that I have known. This connection with our Father in heaven is a delightful, magnificent, lovely thing because he is absolutely delightful, magnificent and lovely. And again, he loves us, which is why we have become his children in the first place. As we grow ever more like Jesus, our divine Brother, we also grow ever more in likeness to our heavenly Father, who is God and who is love. In Christ's interaction with Philip in John 14:8-9, Philip said to him, "Lord, show us the Father, and it is enough for us." Jesus said to him, "Have I been with you so long, and you still do not know me, Philip? Whoever has seen me has seen the Father. How can you say, 'Show us the Father'? Jesus bears such a resemblance to the Father that to know him, to closely observe him, is to see the Father as well. And this likeness will somehow one day be ours in all its fullness.

Once again from 1 John 3, "Beloved, we are God's children now, and what we will be has not yet appeared; but we know that when he appears we shall be like him, because we shall see him as he is." My longing to be like a father, as I have stated, runs very deep. It may be natural, but it is not necessarily healthy if taken to an extreme. Imitation of any mere human can take a detrimental turn toward obsession or infatuation and get perilously close to idolatry. But to be like Jesus, who is so much like the Father, is a holy desire; to see Jesus is to see the Father, to be like Jesus is to be like the Father.

Becoming More Like Him

Someday we will be like Jesus and share all the family resemblance that the Trinity shares, just in a different way. We are not going to become God, or gods, or "like God" in any spiritually corrupt way that the serpent may have intended when he tempted Eve. It will be in the way that God intended from the moment he created us in his image and likeness. That is what we look forward to, but the verse in our focus seems to put this off into the unknowable, invisible future because it says, "we know that when he appears we shall be like him."

I am all for waiting and watching in eager expectation for Jesus Christ. Maranatha! Come Lord Jesus! I long to "see him as he is," knowing that I will be more like him on that day than I am today. Surely, moreover, the day is closer than when we first believed. At the same time, I want to experience more and greater transformation in this present life while I am still waiting. If the Holy Spirit is the deposit, the down payment of what is yet to come, we might say that seeing his work within us, making us more like Jesus now, is the evidence that he will complete the work he has started and will fully transform us into the likeness of Christ. Happily, that is exactly what 1 John 3 promises in not so many words.

"And everyone who thus hopes in him purifies himself as he is pure." John is not giving us a thorough discourse on the role of the Holy Spirit in the sanctification of believers here. Going by the principle that Scripture interprets Scripture, we will attempt to harmonize our verse with other passages rather than taking it on its own. One that comes quickly to mind is Phil 2:12-13, "Therefore, my beloved, as you have always obeyed, so now, not only as in my presence but much more in my absence, work out your own salvation with fear and trembling, for it is God who works in you, both to will and to work for his good pleasure." We work it out in our real-time, real-world context, while he works in us, developing the desires and ability we need to will and to work toward that ultimate, sanctified end. I am also reminded of Eph 4:1-3:

> I therefore, a prisoner for the Lord, urge you to walk in a manner worthy of the calling to which you have been called, with all humility and gentleness, with patience, bearing with one another in love, eager to main-

tain the unity of the Spirit in the bond of peace. There is one body and one Spirit—just as you were called to the one hope that belongs to your call— one Lord, one faith, one baptism, one God and Father of all, who is over all and through all and in all. But grace was given to each one of us according to the measure of Christ's gift.

This passage, like the one in Philippians, puts an emphasis on effort while at the same time reminding us of God's Spirit who completes the work. We walk worthy of our calling. We are eager to maintain the unity of the body, but that unity is of the Spirit, who inhabits the body (of Christ, in this case) and causes it to come together behind the scenes. We work, but it is his work inside of us that enables our work in the first place. So, when John says that we purify ourselves, we can assume he is speaking of how it seems to us, from our perspective. We may never completely grasp what part the Spirit plays in the process, but we can imagine.

Prior to coming to Christ, we probably never considered Christlikeness a desirable goal. We may have occasionally tried to *turn over a new leaf* or make a new start of some kind. New Year's resolutions are one example. Those annual exercises in futility also illustrate just how terrible most of us are at self-improvement. If only a sizable fraction of the self-help books on the market really helped as much as they hoped to, we would already be living in a better world, filled with better people and the whole industry might have worked, written and self-motivated itself right out of a job. Enter the Spirit of God.

The Spirit indwells us and informs us that we are God's children. As we understand from Rom 8:16, "The Spirit himself bears witness with our spirit that we are children of God." We long to be made more into his likeness, to be marked with that family resemblance to our Father that has always been visible with Jesus, but not yet with us. Consequently, we work toward it, purifying ourselves even as he is pure. We are working out our salvation while God works within us, making us more like him.

God the Father has made us his children because he loves us. "See what kind of love the Father has given to us, that we should be called children of God; and so we are." A similar love may or may not have been there for my mother Frances, living with her stepfather, her mother's only husband, Józef Kościołek. I cannot fully understand to what extent it was even true for me, living in my adopted home with a father who probably tried his best while I was little, but then died. Now in Christ, we have been welcomed into a lasting Father-child relationship, which binds us to him eternally while simultaneously separating us from the world.

This world may not know us, but no matter, for we now know God and we long to be like him. We will be thoroughly like him when Jesus comes, and we see our Savior face-to-face. The family resemblance will then be shared by all who presently call him Lord. For now, we can try, relying on the power of the Spirit, to make progress in that direction. We purify our impure selves even as he is pure. The transformation may be grueling and gradual, but it is real. It is not a New Year's resolution or a day trip across the Niagara onto foreign soil. It is rather an enduring, slow but sure development, made possible by a love that longs to make us in its likeness.

The fatherless child's wish has come true, and its granting turns out to be more and better than the child could ever wish for. It is personal. I know my Father, though I desire to know him better, and I hope that you know him too. His love is greater, and we can be sure that he is more of a Father than we have ever dreamed. And one wonderful byproduct of this glorious, newfound relationship is that we can and will be like him. We may be advancing only in increments, but we are advancing. That process has begun even now, thanks to our adoption into the family of God. What more might we consider from the fatherless child's perspective? One connection that I have sometimes pondered is that between fatherhood, abandonment, and adoption.

CHAPTER 4
FATHERHOOD, ABANDONMENT AND ADOPTION

"Wherever I am I know that you will come and see me... But at least you will believe that I was never before so eager to cling to every bit of our old home life and to see you. I know I have often been far from what I should be in my relation to you, and have undervalued an affection and generosity which an experience of "other people's parents" has shown me in a new light. But, please God, I shall do better in the future. Come and see me, I am homesick, that is the long and the short of it."
– C. S. Lewis, in a letter to his father dated 20 June 1918, written from a London hospital. He was recovering from wounds received in battle during WWI. His father never came.

    C. S. "Jack" Lewis lost his mother Flora to cancer when he was child. His father Albert might have taken the opportunity to draw close to his sons, but alas, he failed to do so. Instead, two weeks later, Albert sent Jack and Warnie on an overnight steamer from Northern Ireland to England, where they entered boarding school. They were never really able to draw close to their father again. Alister McGrath describes their departure. "An emotionally unintelligent father bade his emotionally neglected sons an emotionally inadequate farewell. Everything that gave the young Lewis his security and identity seemed to be vanishing around him." [2] Lewis's father-son story seems especially severe, but we can only guess how often it is echoed in our father-starved world.

I cannot claim to be the spokesman for such a large company of people, but I believe that many, maybe most children who experience the lack of a father find themselves struggling with issues related to abandonment. We can hear it in Lewis's letter so many years after he left his father behind at the Belfast port. The extent to which someone will experience such pain can vary widely, so I am not even sure how helpful it is to generalize. But it is valuable to be aware of the issue and to consider its effect on a person's personality. If that person happens to be you, then your personality may be affected.

Abandonment may prompt a wide variety of personal responses, and not all of them are voluntary. I am not trying to shift blame or remove personal responsibility if any of those responses are defective. Difficulties or obstacles in early life do not somehow uncontrollably push a person in extreme directions. All of that said, the pattern is common enough to be worth noting. The experience of poorly adjusted adoptees like myself is both related and relevant.

It took until I was well into adulthood to realize that I was walking around with an underlying layer of stress. Other people and certainly those closest to me may have seen it and known that something was not quite right. But self-understanding can be difficult, and it was especially difficult for me. It was only later, after being exposed to some literature on the family dynamics of adoptive situations that my own situation began to reveal itself. For example, my emotional range was far too limited and too prone to excess in negative directions. In short, I was a textbook example of an adult adoptee's possible problems.

It now makes sense that some of my underlying stress was precisely related to being somehow deserted by someone early on, as early as can be. I may have thought about my birth parents, but this was more in the realm of fantasy. The awareness of the stress

2 Alister McGrath. *C. S. Lewis: A Life: Eccentric Genius, Reluctant Prophet.* (Carol Stream, Tyndale, 2013), 24.

only happened when I allowed myself to consider my heritage, my origins, whatever relatives I might have and how I would potentially fit into that family. It was then that the stress became more obvious because if everything was normal a mere consideration of one's origins should not have produced much stress at all. Further, the familiarity of the negative feelings that I could not name made it obvious that the stress was there all along. The absence of any knowledge of those things made me feel insecure, but it was an insecurity that was for most of my life unacknowledged.

I would surmise that this is true for many others. When they know for a fact that they are in some way fatherless, parentless, or given away, there can be a basic sense that abandonment is just around the corner again. Once bitten, twice shy. The child who has experienced something this traumatic may grow into an adult who reflexively expects to experience similar trauma again and again.

We may assume that other people will leave us or turn against us, whether that is realistic or not. We can then almost involuntarily project this into our relationship with God, as if God is likely to abandon us or cannot be relied upon to remain faithful. Psalm 27:9-10 expresses this sentiment well:

> Hide not your face from me.
> Turn not your servant away in anger,
> O you who have been my help.
> Cast me not off; forsake me not,
> O God of my salvation!
> For my father and my mother have forsaken me,
> but the LORD will take me in.

The average reader may pass over this assuming it is exaggeration or hyperbole. The psalmist is simply being expressive by saying more than needs to be said. But for some of us, the abandonment is real. The inner voice goes something like this, "Where is my mother? Who is my father? I am glad that someone or anyone has taken the time to take care of me, but how certain or long-lasting is that care likely to be? It seems abundantly realistic that I will be abandoned in the end, maybe even by God. Oh God, please don't be like other people!"

Christopher Wright's comments on this passage are insightful (emphasis mine):

> It is unlikely that Psalm 27:10 means that the writer has actually been literally disowned by his human parents. Rather, he probably contemplates the pain of such a devastating disgrace hypothetically as *the worst possible exacerbation* of his feeling of standing alone against the world. If even his parents should turn against him! But in turning to God, as he does through the whole psalm, he knows he is turning to the one whose loving commitment to him is stronger even than the strongest human bond of parent and child. God is the Father who, if ever the believer should be left effectively fatherless, will adopt him as his own and take him in … God is Father to those who have lost the natural bonds of human protection whether because of rejection, or because of natural bereavement.[3]

God is not often compared in the Old Testament with a human father, but in this case where he is, we are told that God will step in when the father is unwilling to be there for the child. When we are forsaken even by our parents, God will take their place.

It takes faith for anyone to believe this about God, and even greater faith to allow it to shape us deep inside. It takes a still higher degree of faith or a deeper degree of trust for the fatherless child. In my own case, for decades of Christian experience, I took these words at face value and would have effortlessly said I believed them. I did not believe them sincerely. At the risk of sounding cliché, I understood them in my head without allowing them into my heart. My heart, I now realize, did not have much of a trust compartment in which to place them. I thought I trusted God as much as one could, but much later something dawned on

3 Christopher J. H. Wright. *Knowing God the Father Through the Old Testament, Knowing God Through the Old Testament Set.* (Downers Grove: IVP Academic, 2007). 36-37

me. The trust that I placed in God was not much different or better than the trust I placed in any human, which wasn't very much. Many people deserved more trust than I gave them. God deserved even so much more than that. He is not like other people.

Everyone is betrayed or abandoned at some point by someone and accordingly must endure at least low-grade experiences of abandonment. Let's call them *normal* experiences. A family member might die, a friend moves away, or a youthful crush ends up being one-sided. These things are also experienced by the fatherless, but they serve to greatly compound the gaping lack of trust that the fatherless child feels as her baseline level. As a result, they seem a greater hardship to the fatherless than they do to other people. Each minor trauma of betrayal, which might interfere with anyone's trust capabilities in the best of cases, becomes part of the reinforcing framework for an internal belief system that is founded mainly on disbelief. That internal system's internal voice can go so far as to say something like, "No one at all should ever be trusted again."

I suspect people who are abandoned by their spouses can feel something similar. It is a major kind of tragedy, and it is felt with a full, life-altering force. The difference here is that when the abandonment occurs early enough, as in childhood, it works its way into the mind (or perhaps more truly, the *brain*) as part of a reality that does not seem like it was ever learned or knowingly experienced. It is the reality that has always been there, the only reality that really exists, or so it seems. As Wright rightly puts it, the psalmist "contemplates the pain of such a devastating disgrace hypothetically as the worst possible exacerbation of his feeling of standing alone against the world." And yet for many of us, the disgrace is not hypothetical.

Nonetheless, the psalmist's response is the right one. Cry out to God rather than let your underlying fears get the best of you. Another response available to the abandoned child is to just deal with it all on your own. This might be expressed as a thought process that says, "If no one wants to stay connected to me, then so what? Who needs connections? If I am, through no choice of my own, unattached to others, perhaps attachment is simply overrated." And so, the fatherless child finds it more and more difficult to attach and is less and less likely to be motivated by an internal need for attachment. A world with as few others as possible and, if possible, a world without God, doesn't seem so bad.

That last statement about a world without God, I am aware, goes against certain widely held Freud-friendly views that say religious belief is somehow based on an inner need for a father figure. In other words, we indulge in the fantasy of faith in a personal God as a form of cosmic wish-fulfillment. We want a father, so we create one in our mind and call him God. Philosophers like Feuerbach and Marx have pushed the theory. People made this stuff up, the story goes, because they wanted such things to be so. Marx gave us the phrase *opium of the people* to describe religion.[4] Some people who suffer use opium to alleviate the pain. In Marx's view, most others turn to religion; it makes them feel better, but mainly by numbing their minds like opium. Such ideas remain popular today though they may be said differently. They seem to have even grown in popularity, to have become mainstream rather than radical.

Personal experience makes it easier for me to agree with a Polish-American poet named Czesław Miłosz (no need to pronounce it correctly), who disagreed with Marx. He concluded, "A true opium for the people is a belief in nothingness after death—the huge solace of thinking that for our betrayals, greed, cowardice, murders we are not going to be judged,"[5] What Miłosz believed intuitively was backed up and documented by Paul C. Vitz, Professor Emeritus of Psychology at NYU. He examined the lives and beliefs of numerous prominent atheists with Feuerbach, Freud, and Marx among them. His discoveries, published in a book called *Faith of the Fatherless,* can be summarized quickly. "[W]hatever might weaken or harm the relationship of a child with his father or parents will in general predispose the child in

---

4 Marx, Karl. *A Contribution to the Critique of Hegel's Philosophy of Right.* Written 1843. Edited by Joseph O'Malley. Translated by Annette Jolin, & Joseph O'Malley. Cambridge University Press, 1970.
5 Miłosz, Czesław. "The Discreet Charm of Nihilism." *The New York Review of Books,* November 1998.

adulthood to atheism or unbelief or to spiritualist beliefs without a personal God."[6] Lousy father-child relationships often lead to a lousy or non-existent relationship with God. And several big-name atheists seem to prove the point.

In other words, the abandoned child can learn to deal with abandonment, but not always in helpful ways. If it seems to you that emotional distance from others is a constant reality, then growing too close to people or too close to God can be difficult or even frightening. It seems both impossible and undesirable, and therefore is not given sufficient effort. This is a choice in some mysterious way, but it is a choice camouflaged to the orphan's own mind and heart by a lack of his or her own experience. Lack of first-hand experience leads to inadequate attention resulting in a blank space enclosed by a layer of unbelief. The fatherless child feels alone and, we might say, just *knows* that such isolation is exactly how life is. This is, to the fatherless mind, the only way the world, the universe, or any possible universe can ever be. That child, regardless of age and maybe in adulthood, needs to learn that sometimes what we "know" is not true, or is at least not the full story. The trick is to try to see more.

If atheism is the "faith of the fatherless" as Vitz put it, then a sincere effort to put faith in our heavenly Father is the defining struggle of the fatherless believer in God. Psalm 68:5 says, "Father of the fatherless and protector of widows, is God in his holy habitation." Can we believe this and receive it as applying to us? Are we willing to look to God in the agony of our abandonment and believe that he truly does care? When we are tempted to channel our lack of faith in others toward a perfectly and infinitely faithful Creator, are we willing to say that these negative sentiments of ours are understandable, but still unwarranted or misguided? Have we been tempted to blame God for our trouble when in fact we should allow our pain to direct us toward him?

One of my favorite observations by C. S. Lewis, the abandoned child, who as we have seen knew something about pain, is

---

6 Vitz, Paul C. *Faith of the Fatherless: The Psychology of Atheism*. Kindle. (San Francisco: Ignatius Press, 2013), Kindle location 481.

"God whispers to us in our pleasures, speaks in our conscience, but shouts in our pain: it is His megaphone to rouse a deaf world"[7] If we let it, our deepest heartaches can act as a reminder that God is still there and that he cares and that he is waiting to receive us to himself. A little further on in the same book, Lewis elaborates, expressing himself in a hard truth:

> While what we call "our own life" remains agreeable we will not surrender it to Him. What then can God do in our interests but make "our own life" less agreeable to us, and take away the plausible source of false happiness? It is just here, where God's providence seems at first to be most cruel, that the Divine humility, the stooping down of the Highest, most deserves praise.[8]

Abandonment is always painful. Abandonment in childhood is normally worse. And it is precisely here that we may see that life is not only "less agreeable," but an unprotected shock moving toward a defenseless horror when we stop to consider it. False happiness is not available when happiness of any kind is hard to find. Why would God allow something as cruel as the longing of a fatherless child? I do not say this next statement lightly, but rather with sober, deliberate consideration: *He may allow it, as one of many types of tragedy in a fallen world, to show that his mercy, grace, compassion, and love are all greater on the scale of marvelous wonder than the worst evils are on the scale of awfulness.*

In 2 Cor 4:8-9, Paul offers a laundry list of trials that have not yet defeated Christ's servants, "We are afflicted in every way, but not crushed; perplexed, but not driven to despair; persecuted, but not forsaken; struck down, but not destroyed," etc. A bit later, in 4:17, he reveals a larger point. "For this light momentary affliction is preparing for us an eternal weight of glory beyond all comparison." Once again, we are afflicted in every way, perplexed, persecuted, and struck down, but not ultimately forsaken by God.

---

7 Lewis, C. S. *The Problem of Pain*. Kindle. New York: HarperCollins, 1996. 92
8 Lewis, *The Problem of Pain*. 95

And if we could weigh this affliction and see it as it really is, we would know that it is truly *light* and *momentary*. It is small and temporary. It may not seem so to us, especially in the midst of our trials, but that is only because we do not yet comprehend what "an eternal weight of glory beyond all comparison" even means. The beauty is above our understanding. The deep permanence and magnificence of it is something beyond our finite grasp. Our imagination is too tiny to define eternal glory, let alone see it as something that is ours. But that is what God offers as an adoptive Father in search of the fatherless child.

God offers a heavy-duty, glorious, durable belonging in place of the rejection we have experienced. Have we been deserted by those who should have taken responsibility for us from the start? If so, God stands in their place and receives us, and we will belong to him forever. We are chosen by him, and he will never go back on that decision. Our status in God's family is secure and the future looks better than the past. Being chosen by God is far more mysterious and wonderful than even being chosen by human adoptive parents.

What does it mean to be *chosen* by parents here on earth? I cannot truly say how common it is these days, but in times past people in the adoption world used to speak of a child being "chosen" by his or her adoptive parents. One example of this strategy to make the child feel wanted is the book *The Chosen Baby*[9] It is a picture book explaining that adopted children are chosen by, rather than born to, their parents. There is an encouraging truth in this perspective to be sure, but it is required by its very emphasis to downplay the fact that the "chosen" child was first abandoned by the original parents. Left unexplored in this book and this perspective are some crucial facts. There is an untold story of a father, often unknown to his offspring, who may have abandoned both mother and child. There is a mother whose finite abilities prevented her from giving in to her own maternal instinct to care for her infant. She gave her child away and may have been convinced

---

9 Valentina Pavlovna Wasson. *The Chosen Baby*. Second ed. Philadelphia: Lippincott Williams & Wilkins, 1977.

that this was for the child's own good. There is a sense in which this child knows he was unplanned, unwanted, unexpected, never meant to be, or *something*. In short, a mistake.

The adoptive parents' choosing of the child, while admirable in many ways, is not simply a positive, altruistic action. It is also a way to correct the original error. It is an important *addition to*, but not a *replacement for*, the original narrative. With God's help, it can be a wonderful addition, and much more than a mere epilogue. It might be the more important part of the story. But it is an addition all the same. God's adopting of us is very different. Consider the complexities of this opening passage of Ephesians:

> Blessed be the God and Father of our Lord Jesus Christ, who has blessed us in Christ with every spiritual blessing in the heavenly places, even as he chose us in him before the foundation of the world, that we should be holy and blameless before him. In love he predestined us for adoption to himself as sons through Jesus Christ, according to the purpose of his will, to the praise of his glorious grace, with which he has blessed us in the Beloved (Eph 1:3-6).

This kind of choosing is something very different indeed. To be chosen in Christ before the foundation of the world brings with it a certainty, a stability, and an unconditional acceptance the likes of which mere humans cannot bestow. In other words, in the infinite ages before my unnamed father somehow got together with my unfamiliar mother, perhaps never to be heard from again, God chose me. With 20/20 foresight, he looked directly at, and then looked beyond, the sin in which I was conceived. He stared omnisciently at the sins I would later commit, the rebellion, the confusion and the merely human flaws that were mine and decided that I should be holy and blameless before him. He would have to make me so, of course, because he knew that, like all other members of this fallen race, I was defective in myriad ways by nature. Then in love he predestined me to adoption as his own son. This was his plan, his decision, and the outworking of his perfect will.

No sentimental story of a chosen baby or a special child can match this marvelous history. My chosenness was not necessitated by a prior abandonment, nor was it necessary at all. And praise the God of the heavens, it preceded the foundation of the world. Before Adam and Eve ate the forbidden fruit, acquiring knowledge of good and evil, God knew me and wanted me for his own. He loved me before anyone outside the Triune Deity knew what it meant to be loved. Before creation was created, he intended to adopt me as his child so that I would be a permanent part of his family.

In other words, my story did not begin with the abandonment, trauma or parting of ways that resulted in a fatherless child. It began with God the Father writing one story, which would become the actual, true-to-life story, the one he chose out of all possible scenarios, worst-case or best. God personally decided that I would be one of his story's characters. It would be a story full of twists and turns, one of comedy, tragedy, complexity, and drama. There would be increasing tension, prolonged conflict, and incremental examples of partial resolution. And before the end of that story, against all odds, he would see to it that I belonged to him.

The primal abandonment that I or anyone else has ever experienced in our earthly existence was much less primal than God's authorship of the entire tale. Abandonment was an important detail in the telling of my particular story, but not the most important by far. His original intention, which preceded the foundation of the world, was far better and far more foundational than the pain of rejection or all the cruel wickedness that humanity might ever devise. Salvation, or at least God's plan for it, comes before any direct act of sin. Nothing I have done or that has ever been done to me was left out of the original solution to the plentiful problems of our fallen existence.

To think of all that this means, consider Rom 8:14-16, "For all who are led by the Spirit of God are sons of God. For you did not receive the spirit of slavery to fall back into fear, but you have received the Spirit of adoption as sons, by whom we cry, 'Abba! Father!' The Spirit himself bears witness with our spirit that we are children of God." For children who feel like they never quite fit in, this is life-changing. It alters our perception of self in relation to family. If you did not grow up in your family of origin, or some part of that family was missing, it is likely you carried with you a sense that you never quite belonged. I know I did, and I know that I am not alone.

If, however, the very Spirit of God is within us, and is continually reminding us, teaching us, and affirming to us that we are children of God, then we are children of God indeed. If this was God's plan from the very beginning, if we were chosen in Christ before the foundation of the world, then this is the family for which we were made. We *cannot* not fit in. God's created intent for us is fully realized only in the context of our divine adoption. It is no mere afterthought. It is not a Plan B. It is God's original plan, and we find ourselves at the center of it.

Note clearly how this does away with any basic, perceived need to fear. We may not have seen that within us was an underlying fear of abandonment. It was there, we may have felt the stress of it, the tension and apprehension, but we could never name the cause. It was the hypervigilance of the child traumatized through abandonment, now quietly, nervously awaiting the next emotional trauma. That fear, normal though it may seem, can now be gone. We may confidently pray, Lord, help me to focus on the absence of fear. Perfect me and let me experience your perfect love. "There is no fear in love, but perfect love casts out fear. For fear has to do with punishment, and whoever fears has not been perfected in love" (1 John 4:18). Contemplating the love of God for us is critical to the renunciation of our fears.

No family is perfect, at least no *earthly* family is perfect. But for all who know God the Father through Jesus Christ, the eternal family that we belong to will be perfect because God will make it so. Imitations can be better or worse. Families on earth are, at best, the better imitations of our perfect family in heaven. Still, the best, most godly, most loving human family is still but an imperfect reflection of the perfect family of God. The best father on earth is but an imperfect reflection of our perfect Father in heaven.

God ordained at the time of creation that families would be the building blocks of earthly society, or earthly community. At the moment he made the man and the woman in his image and told them to be fruitful and multiply, he was instituting a certain category of relationship. It is one that would be distinguished by closeness, connection, resemblance, and love. Our heavenly family is not a reflection of this. It is not an imitation of this earthly model. It is the other way around. Our earthly family foreshadows what God plans to do in eternity. Likewise, the concept of fatherhood was put into place by God in order to illustrate and explain to us the relationship between the Father and the Son. The family is a teaching tool, used by God to give us a glimpse of what our eternal existence will be like.

Some of us have had better earthly families to look at than others. This will influence us as we try to learn these truths. But even the worst example of a family on earth can be overcome by God making us a part of a more glorious reality, the genuine of which all other families are mere copies. We cannot know all there is to know about fatherhood from having or being an earthly father. Some of us have learned very little, due to real-life experiences of abandonment. Those days will one day be gone. Our adoption into the family of God and our experience of his perfect love in a perfect household with other perfected saints is our destiny. Oh, haste the day.

In our next chapter, we shall examine God's heart toward the orphan. The refreshing news for the fatherless is that with him, abandonment is not an option.

CHAPTER 5
I WILL NOT LEAVE YOU AS ORPHANS

"I had no feeling for him. He did not seem to have anything to do with me. I felt no feeling of fatherhood."
– Ernest Hemingway, *A Farewell to Arms*

In Hemingway's novel, *A Farewell to Arms,* the father, Frederic Henry, has no feelings at all toward his newborn son. It seems that this must be true in many real-world cases, given the absence of a father in so many children's lives. Perhaps that is also how many now-grown children would describe their relationships toward their fathers. The child cannot relate to the father at all or at least not in any constructive way. Whether or not the father is alive, the child feels like a functional orphan. God is different, as we shall see.

We are now going to take a deep dive into the Bible. The Scriptures could not be clearer about how to treat orphans. To any who feel the lack of a father or father figure, this will remind us how God views us in our situation. If you do not feel this lack yourself, you certainly know others who do, so the lessons are still completely relevant. The references below do not contain an exhaustive catalog, but they will give us an idea how consistent and insistent the Bible is when it comes to the treatment of *the fatherless.*

God's severity on this issue may alarm us. Beginning in the law, Exod 2:22-23 issues a command to the newly forming nation of Israel "You shall not mistreat any widow or fatherless child." God supplements the instruction with a threat, "If you do mistreat them, and they cry out to me, I will surely hear their cry, and my wrath will burn, and I will kill you with the sword, and your wives shall become widows and your children fatherless." Those who mistreat the fatherless put themselves in the express lane toward God's judgment.

When we get to Deut 24:17-22, *the fatherless* are again included in those that are eligible for special care:

> You shall not pervert the justice due to the sojourner or to *the fatherless*, or take a widow's garment in pledge, but you shall remember that you were a slave in Egypt and the Lord your God redeemed you from there; therefore I command you to do this.

> When you reap your harvest in your field and forget a sheaf in the field, you shall not go back to get it. It shall be for the sojourner, *the fatherless*, and the widow, that the Lord your God may bless you in all the work of your hands.

> When you beat your olive trees, you shall not go over them again. It shall be for the sojourner, *the fatherless*, and the widow. When you gather the grapes of your vineyard, you shall not strip it afterward. It shall be for the sojourner, *the fatherless*, and the widow. You shall remember that you were a slave in the land of Egypt; therefore I command you to do this.

As we examine the poetry of Israel, Ps 82:3-4 encourages the same:

> Give justice to the weak and the *fatherless*;
> maintain the right of the afflicted and the destitute.
> Rescue the weak and the needy;
> deliver them from the hand of the wicked."

Further, Ps 95:6 offers the opposite as a prime example of evil people at their worst:

> They kill the widow and the sojourner,
> and murder *the fatherless*.

When Job provides evidence for his righteousness, he says in Job 29:11-12:

> When the ear heard, it called me blessed,
> and when the eye saw, it approved,
> because I delivered the poor who cried for help,
> and *the fatherless* who had none to help him.

Indeed, God himself, when telling his people what evidence of repentance would look like, says all this in Isa 1:16-17:

> Wash yourselves; make yourselves clean;
> remove the evil of your deeds from before my eyes;
> cease to do evil,
> learn to do good;
> seek justice,
> correct oppression;
> bring justice to *the fatherless,*
> plead the widow's cause.

As the Old Testament comes to a close, the Lord proclaims his coming judgment. As he gives his reasons for it, in Mal 3:5, oppression of the fatherless is one of the charges named. "Then I will draw near to you for judgment. I will be a swift witness against the sorcerers, against the adulterers, against those who swear falsely, against those who oppress the hired worker in his wages, the widow *and the fatherless*, against those who thrust aside the sojourner, and do not fear me, says the Lord of hosts." All the above emphasize care for orphans, for the fatherless, as one of the chief concerns that God places upon his people. This is not an optional point for a people or a society that hopes in any way to please God.

Those of us who have experienced the loneliness and longing of abandonment often struggle, consciously or unconsciously with whether we can truly trust God. We may easily pay him lip service, but when push comes to shove and we analyze our anxieties, trust levels are low in general, and this includes our trust toward God. Our gut sense is that God cannot be trusted, but he can. We just do not feel it. Of course, we know it in our heads if we are Bible readers and believers, but our doubts challenge the plain meaning of the text. This reveals a need for some extra encouragement.

The main reason I included so many Bible verses in the above section was to provide plenty of evidence that God values care for the fatherless child. He wants his people to care because he cares for the fatherless child himself. He does not issue these commandments to Israel for abstract, indescribable reasons. He wanted the people and the society formed by the nation in its own land to reflect his character, his will, and his deepest desires. That collection of Bible passages was not complete, but it gave us an accurate representation of what God wanted. He wanted such a society because that is the kind of society that would reflect his love.

Here are a few more verses revealing God's character, which is now set before us as the ultimate example of good:

> For the Lord your God is God of gods and Lord of lords, the great, the mighty, and the awesome God, who is not partial and takes no bribe. He executes justice for *the fatherless* and the widow, and loves the sojourner, giving him food and clothing. (Deut 10:17-18)

> O Lord, you hear the desire of the afflicted;
> you will strengthen their heart; you will incline your ear
> to do justice to *the fatherless* and the oppressed,
> so that man who is of the earth may strike terror no more.
> (Ps 10:17-18)

Father of *the fatherless* and protector of widows
is God in his holy habitation.
(Ps 68:5)

The Lord watches over the sojourners;
he upholds the widow *and the fatherless*,
but the way of the wicked he brings to ruin.
(Ps 146:9)

Allow the above collection of verses to sink in. God's position on the fatherless, not to mention the widow and the sojourner, could not be clearer. He demands that his people care for them. If they will not do so, he promises to take their care upon themselves and judge those who oppress them. This is how the God we serve reveals himself to us and has revealed himself from ancient times.

Finally, when we get to the New Testament, James 1:27 lets us know what true piety should look like after Christ and under the New Covenant. "Religion that is pure and undefiled before God the Father is this: to visit orphans and widows in their affliction, and to keep oneself unstained from the world." This verse reminds us that God has not changed. The values and standards that he desired from his people under the Old Covenant are still present, without the law to enforce them, in the New. That brings us around once again to the topic of trust.

Perhaps you have had the experience of knowing full well you can be trusted in a certain situation. Then, without sufficient grounds, someone utterly doubts or questions you precisely where you know they need not do so. I am not speaking at the moment of establishing credibility with a stranger. If we are applying for a job or would like to rent an apartment, we should expect to have to prove ourselves in some way. Nor do I speak here of the normal accountability required in work or relationships. When someone tells their spouse or their boss that they are going to be late, it does not have to be a lack of mutual trust that expects the latecomer to give a reason for their delay. A willingness to maintain credibility can motivate us as easily as the desire to establish it. Nonetheless, when we are forced, perhaps continuously, to defend ourselves under routine circumstances with someone who should know us well enough by now, we may conclude that their lack of trust toward us is unwarranted.

This can make us feel strangely unsettled, insulted, and put on the defensive. When that lack of trust is persistent regardless of what we do to prove ourselves, the relationship starts to become strained. If you have had that happen to you, then you know from experience how unnerving such encounters can be. You begin wondering what has caused this shortage of confidence. If you have not done anything to deserve it, while simultaneously doing things that should allow such confidence to be built, you wonder where to begin to even address what is happening. You can begin doubting yourself and viewing the other person suspiciously.

God, of course, is not going to lose confidence in his own power or goodness due to any lack of faith on our part. Since he knows us perfectly, he is never going to wonder what is going on in our hearts or heads that might bring about our lack of trust. He knows. I draw attention to the feeling a lack of trust induces in the one not trusted because it reminds me of Jesus at any of the many times that he uses the phrase "little faith."

For example, in the Sermon on the Mount, Jesus gives us the example of flowers, compares them to Solomon's clothing, and then says, "But if God so clothes the grass of the field, which today is alive and tomorrow is thrown into the oven, will he not much more clothe you, O you of little faith?" (Matt 6:30).

When he was sleeping during the storm and the disciples woke him, he said to them, "'Why are you afraid, O you of little faith?' Then he rose and rebuked the winds and the sea, and there was a great calm" (Matt 8:26).

As Peter started sinking during a failed attempt at walking on water, "Jesus immediately reached out his hand and took hold of him, saying to him, 'O you of little faith, why did you doubt?' And when they got into the boat, the wind ceased" (Matt 14:31-32).

While again in a boat, at a point after Jesus fed both the 5,000 and the 4,000, he brought up the "leaven of the Pharisees and Sadducees." His disciples did not understand and began a discussion, "But Jesus, aware of this, said, 'O you of little faith, why are you discussing among yourselves the fact that you have no bread? Do you not yet perceive? Do you not remember the five loaves for the five thousand, and how many baskets you gathered? Or the seven loaves for the four thousand, and how many baskets you gathered? How is it that you fail to understand that I did not speak about bread? (Matt 16:8-11). Jesus, as God, can always be trusted, and he expected his disciples to keep this in mind.

Regardless of our experience with other people, despite any early and frequent violations of our trust, we need to remember that God truly can be trusted. He is patient as he works with us to build that trust, but he most certainly intends to build it. There will then come points when we need act upon our acquired intimacy with him and view him with something much like the confidence that he truly deserves. Are there risks involved? Yes, but life is inherently risky and so is faith in God. There are risks involved in all kinds of relationships.

Canadian professor John Stackhouse observes, "We already are accustomed to taking the greatest of relational risks in this life, whether trusting a spouse or trusting a surgeon or trusting a rescuer. And we simply must perform the same exercise of trust in religious matters as well, as human beings who recognize that we do not and cannot know all before deciding." [10] This is the kind of trust we need to exercise in God. Once we admit that our relationship with him ought to be more important than any other, we should then be willing to take the next step. Our knowledge of God and our trust level will increase as we do.

Eventually, we shall be able to take God at his word when the Bible speaks of his care for the fatherless or the orphan. Will we know how each and every circumstance or situation will turn out before we place our trust in God? Can we be sure that we will never feel, or even truly be, abandoned again? No, not on the human level, at least. But that is simply part of exercising any faith at all

---

10 John G. Stackhouse, Jr. *Can God Be Trusted? Faith and the Challenge of Evil.* Second Edition. (Downers Grove: IVP Academic, 2009). 192

while living in fallen world. We need to look beyond our difficulties, our feelings, and at times even our tragic circumstances and place our trust in him. He will not leave us as orphans.

The night before he died, Jesus reassured his disciples using these exact words in John 14:18, "I will not leave you as orphans; I will come to you." The disciples were all grown men, not little children, when Jesus said this. What Jesus understood was that they had come to rely upon and take comfort in his presence so much that his absence would feel much like childhood abandonment. This is reassuring in at least two ways.

First, Jesus is expressing the continuously established character of God at a time when these early apostles needed it most. He is not in the business of abandonment. He knows what his personal presence means to his followers. He has created us with a need for him and he is not going to relinquish us now, leaving us to our own devices and placing us at the mercy of the world. For Jesus, abandonment is not an option.

Second, these disciples are grown men, but they still needed the reassuring presence of Christ. He never intended them to take on their new life and ministry without him. Likewise, we should never imagine ourselves to be able to take on our responsibilities alone. Any sense that we as adults ought to be able to take on the challenges of the world with no one to watch out for us is misguided. It could be American or western individualism. It might also be something we have learned to do because of early or repeated desertion by those who almost certainly should have cared. Either way, it is not Christ who expects us to fly solo through the turbulence of life. He will not leave us as orphans, because that would go completely against his nature. As he promised his disciples, "I will come to you," but what does his coming to them mean?

Most immediately, it probably had something to do with his resurrection appearances. Confused, dejected and grieving, it is hard to even imagine the feeling of suddenly seeing their rabbi alive. They had witnessed his cruel execution. They had seen the bloody and beaten corpse and they knew that Joseph of Arimathea had taken it and put it in his own tomb. That kind of shock leaves a lasting impression – one that they would not get over for a very long time. Unless, of course, Jesus himself could undo the whole experience by conquering death itself. It turns out that is exactly what he did. Their exhilaration is hard to imagine, since we have never experienced anything quite like it, but there is more.

Before his death and resurrection, while still in the midst of that farewell discourse, Jesus said, "A little while, and you will see me no longer; and again a little while, and you will see me" (John 16:16). As was often the case, the disciples did not immediately understand his words, so he went on to say, in John 16:20-22:

> Truly, truly, I say to you, you will weep and lament, but the world will rejoice. You will be sorrowful, but your sorrow will turn into joy. When a woman is giving birth, she has sorrow because her hour has come, but when she has delivered the baby, she no longer remembers the anguish, for joy that a human being has been born into the world. So also you have sorrow now, but I will see you again, and your hearts will rejoice, and no one will take your joy from you.

Jesus compares the joy of his resurrection to the birth of a child. His matter-of-fact assertion highlights the abnormal lack of feeling in Hemingway's character at the birth of his son. Normally, when a woman is in labor, the pain is intense, but it is only temporary. The effects of childbirth, namely the joy of the presence of the child, are lasting. For some of us, the evidence may be mixed as to whether our own birth really caused that much joy to our mothers, but that does not negate Jesus' point. Each of us is living proof that labor pains are not the point of pregnancy. Children are, and whatever joy each child brings into the world supersedes the pain of childbirth. In the same way, the risen Christ supersedes the sorrow surrounding his death. While the disciples could always look back on that experience to motivate them, we cannot. For the rest of us, Jesus promised something – or rather, someone – more, so that we would have an experience that we can share equally with them. He promised the presence of the Holy Spirit.

The coming and abiding presence of the Holy Spirit of God is a better replacement for the orphaned life than the personal presence of the post-resurrection Jesus. Though clearly not as limited as we are, he was still limited by some human boundaries. Christ was still available only in one place at one time with one set of people. Since Christ ascended to his Father and sent the Helper to be with us, we, just as much as the apostles, experience Christ's presence today.

In John 14:16-17, Jesus gave his disciples this promise, "And I will ask the Father, and he will give you another Helper, to be with you forever, even the Spirit of truth, whom the world cannot receive, because it neither sees him nor knows him. You know him, for he dwells with you and will be in you." The Holy Spirit's presence with us is lasting.

A bit later, in John 16:6-7, Christ remarks, "But because I have said these things to you, sorrow has filled your heart. Nevertheless, I tell you the truth: it is to your advantage that I go away, for if I do not go away, the Helper will not come to you. But if I go, I will send him to you." It is to our advantage, it is better for us, to have the Holy Spirit than the physical presence of Christ. He is another Helper, much like Jesus, and is with us forever. This is a satisfying replacement for the abandonment the orphan or anyone else can feel. The Spirit is, in some strange way, the very presence of Christ.

Without going into an overly long discourse on the relationships within the Trinity, consider what Paul says in Rom 8:9-10. There he makes this comment on the Holy Spirit, "You, however, are not in the flesh but in the Spirit, if in fact the Spirit of God dwells in you. Anyone who does not have the Spirit of Christ does not belong to him. But if Christ is in you, although the body is dead because of sin, the Spirit is life because of righteousness." In this short passage, the apostle calls the Holy Spirit "the Spirit," and then "the Spirit of God." He later calls this same Spirit "the Spirit of Christ," and soon after he says, "if Christ is in you." All of this is to say that if the Holy Spirit indwells us as believers (and he does), then Christ indwells us as well. Therefore Paul, in Col 1:27, can speak of "Christ in you, the hope of glory."

The more we allow ourselves to think about this remarkable truth, the more utterly amazed we should be. Christ was once with his disciples, as was the Holy Spirit. Now, by means of the Holy Spirit's presence, both dwell within all disciples as part of our new life in Christ. "Whoever keeps his commandments abides in God, and God in him. And by this we know that he abides in us, by the Spirit whom he has given us" (1 John 3:24). God is with us and in us, and he has no plans to leave.

When Moses pushed back against God sending him to Pharoah, the promise was much the same. "But Moses said to God, 'Who am I that I should go to Pharaoh and bring the children of Israel out of Egypt?' He said, 'But I will be with you …'" (Exod 3:11-12). When God sent Joshua over the Jordan to claim the Promised Land, we see the same promise again, "Have I not commanded you? Be strong and courageous. Do not be frightened, and do not be dismayed, for the Lord your God is with you wherever you go" (Joshua 1:9). Now we have the word of the Savior himself, speaking to his disciples and through them to us.

He will not leave us as orphans; nor will he leave us at all. We can count on his comforting, empowering presence right up until that day when we see him face to face. That day is not so far away. "Besides this, you know the time, that the hour has come for you to wake from sleep. For salvation is nearer to us now than when we first believed. The night is far gone; the day is at hand. So then let us cast off the works of darkness and put on the armor of light" (Rom 13:11-12). The time is short, and as Jesus has said, "And behold, I am with you always, to the end of the age" (Matt 28:20). This declaration should bring comfort to every believer. We are never truly alone.

The fatherless child within me appreciates this promise. It is perfectly consistent and perfectly in tune with the character of God, who can never stop thinking of the orphan. As I age out of anything remotely connected to childhood, I am even more comforted by the promise of Jesus in John 14:18, who left his disciples with the words, "I will not leave you as orphans; I will come to you." Now, knowing that I enjoy the presence of God within me, through the Person of God's Holy Spirit, I am, or at least I am able to be, the most deeply comforted of all. I need not worry about God leaving me at any point in my future. There is a confidence available to me that I have only begun to delight in. Bring on the next challenge and God will be with me – and with you if you are willing. From the difficulties of childhood to the trials of old age, our Lord will never leave.

This fact should cause us great comfort, but that does not mean it will do so without a little practice or intention from our side. This brings us to our next reflection, which involves working toward an untroubled heart.

CHAPTER 6
WORKING TOWARD
AN UNTROUBLED HEART

*"Thou hast made us for thyself, O Lord, and our heart
is restless until it finds its rest in thee."*
– Augustine of Hippo, *Confessions*

In John 14:1, Jesus makes the statement, "Let not your hearts be troubled. Believe in God; believe also in me." He repeats himself not long after in John 14:27, putting some of the same words in the context of his peace. "Peace I leave with you; my peace I give to you. Not as the world gives do I give to you. Let not your hearts be troubled, neither let them be afraid." Our faith in Christ needs to relate to several things. First, our relationship with God as Father. Second, our faith in Christ as God on the same level as God the Father. Third, the personal experience of God-given heavenly peace. And fourth, an untroubled heart.

Our Relationship with God as Father

When we put our faith in Christ, we are accepting the fact that God is our Father. In John 17:3, as Jesus prays, he says, "And this is eternal life, that they know you, the only true God, and Jesus Christ whom you have sent." What Christ is saying is that the eternal life that we receive by faith in him is defined by the new relationship that we have with the Father and the Son. We know God and his Son Jesus Christ, and that somehow *is* eternal life, which needs to be understood as both a quantity and a quality of life.

First, eternal life can be described as everlasting or *never-ending* or using some other such term that means it will keep on going and will not stop. I emphasize this point first because we sometimes hear Christians focus on eternal life as a *quality* of life *as opposed to* a quantity of life. I understand why. It is possible to misunderstand eternal life as being much like the life we have now, complete with its troubles and our imperfections, just without end. That is surely not what Jesus meant. But if we say it is a quality of life *rather than* a quantity, then we are not doing justice to the term *eternal.* Jesus could have easily substituted some other term unrelated to time (*most excellent* or *super wonderful*?) if he did not mean for time to be involved at all. So, we must be careful not to fall into a false dichotomy. It is not an either/or situation; it is a both/and thing. God is eternal; that is one of his attributes, but we are not, since we are created beings. He can, however, give us life everlasting if he wishes, and he does if the Bible is to be believed. This life is acquired by an intimate connection with him, facilitated by the Holy Spirit who regenerates us and gives us new life in Christ.

Second, we must speak of this new life as qualitatively different from the mere earthly life we were born with. We have come to know the only true God and Jesus Christ, his Son, the One sent here for our salvation. Prior to this, we did not know God at all. We may have known of him, in a fact-knowing kind of way. We may have believed that there was a God. This is often true of people who come to know God personally. They come to believe in God in the abstract on the way to a personal faith. It was certainly true in my case. Growing up Catholic exposed me thoroughly to the idea of God, even if he sometimes seemed distant or hard to understand. But to know God personally and to know him as our Father is a vastly different thing indeed. It is so radically and fundamentally life-changing that it is one of the thoughts behind this entire book.

For those of us, for example, the fatherless, who are not always sure what to even make of the fatherly relationship, this idea of eternal life can be a helpful reference point. Just think. Our relationship with God the Father is integral to eternal life itself. He is the only true God, the only God there is, and a God "who never lies" (Titus 1:2). Paul's words to Titus reinforce this idea when he speaks of "knowledge of the truth, which accords with godliness, in hope of eternal life, which God, who never lies, promised before the ages began (Titus 1:1-2). Our knowledge of the truth, knowledge of God and the hope of eternal life are all interconnected. We need to live in this reality constantly, washing our hearts and minds with a continuous stream of Scripture, in order to learn to appreciate what this actually means. As we absorb the text of the Bible and let it flow through us, our relationship with God will intensify. No, we will not get any more of eternal life than we have already. We already own it all right now. But we will grow in our experience of it. We will grow in our understanding of what it means to know God, and in this knowing of him, we will know better what it means to have eternal life. This life is ours in knowing the Father and the Son. We have talked a little about the Father but let's now talk about the Son.

Our Faith in Christ as God on the Same Level as God the Father

Another way we get to know our Father is by examining the life of the Son. In John 14:8-9, "Philip said to him, 'Lord, show us the Father, and it is enough for us.' Jesus said to him, 'Have I been with you so long, and you still do not know me, Philip? Whoever has seen me has seen the Father. How can you say, 'Show us the Father'?" We may not appreciate this statement by Jesus as much as we should. Once we look at Jesus, we need not feel that God the Father is somehow distant, detached, or unavailable. Nor should we imagine that Jesus is somehow less than truly God. Such is the reality of believing in Jesus who says, "Believe in God; believe also in me." It is understanding the truth of Christ's declaration, "And this is eternal life, that they know you, the only true God, and Jesus Christ whom you have sent."

As we read through the Gospels and read about Jesus, does it occur to us that his character is the character of the Father? They are one (John 10:30). His will was so in line with the Father's will that he could say, "My food is to do the will of him who sent me and to accomplish his work" (John 4:34). He found life-giving nourishment in doing the Father's will. More than that, he could say, "When you have lifted up the Son of Man, then you will know that I am he, and that I do nothing on my own authority, but speak just as the Father taught me. And he who sent me is with me. He has not left me alone, for I always do the things that are pleasing to him" (John 8:28-29). When we look at the works of Jesus, we are seeing exactly what the Father would do in all those situations. When we listen to the words of Jesus, we are hearing what the Father would say. We are wise to remind ourselves of this, not only because we may not always make the connection, but because many who have it wrong might try to confuse us with their ideas.

In Brian McLaren's *The Story We Find Ourselves In,* the characters are having a conversation about the cross. One of them, an Australian-American named Kerry, has questions, "For starters," she says, "If God wants to forgive us, why doesn't he just do it? How does punishing an innocent person make things better? That just sounds like one more injustice in the cosmic equation. It sounds like divine child abuse. You know?"[11] The Father, in Kerry's view (though I hope not in McLaren's) would seem to be venting his wrath on his innocent Son, as if the Father and the Son were not in complete agreement that this should be the case.

What we just read above, about the unity of the Father and the Son, and the Son's willing obedience to the Father, should put all such thoughts to rest. At best, they are a gross misunderstanding of what was taking place. The Father and Son were working together to express their great love for us. At worst, they are blasphemous. It also puts Jesus somehow at odds with his Father, which is a picture we never actually get from the Gospels. They both love one another, and they both love us.

---

11 Brian D. McLaren, *The Story We Find Ourselves In: Further Adventures of a New Kind of Christian*, (San Francisco, Jossy-Bass, 2003), 102.

Consider John 3:16, which used to be better known than it is now. "For God so loved the world, that he gave his only Son, that whoever believes in him should not perish but have eternal life." Then consider this somewhat longer, less famous passage:

> So Jesus said to them, "Truly, truly, I say to you, the Son can do nothing of his own accord, but only what he sees the Father doing. For whatever the Father does, that the Son does likewise. For the Father loves the Son and shows him all that he himself is doing. And greater works than these will he show him, so that you may marvel. For as the Father raises the dead and gives them life, so also the Son gives life to whom he will. (John 5:19-21)

This kind of unity exists between the Father and the Son because they are both equally God. Sure, we know that the Son always does the will of the Father while we do not read of the Father always doing the will of the Son. But that does not make Jesus any less God; it only makes him submissive or subordinate to the Father's will. A loving, obedient son is no less human than his loving, human father. Loving obedience does not make Jesus any less God.

To conclude the thought of the complete deity of the Son, let us remember two things. First, Jesus is the clearest picture of God the Father that we have available to us. Look at his life and we see what the Father would look like if, somehow, he too took on human form. But he did not; Jesus did that. And second, Jesus is God, on the same level as God the Father. He did not exchange deity for humanity. He added humanity to deity, a deity that remained unchanged.

The Personal Experience of God-given Heavenly Peace

Again, in John 14:27, Jesus says to his disciples, "Peace I leave with you; my peace I give to you. Not as the world gives do I give to you. Let not your hearts be troubled, neither let them be afraid." The world's peace is mainly based on circumstances. We feel it when things are going our way or when our favorite markers of safety and security are in place. The problem with that kind of peace is that it is, by its very definition, temporary. Things do not always go our way. Those favorite markers of security that we have – like our health, our environment, or our bank account – these things can and do sway back and forth or bounce up and down and then what? The world's peace sways and bounces with them. It flies out the window and we no longer feel secure. No peace.

I can vividly remember the day my adopted father died. It was in June, near the end of the school year when I was 13 and I came home from school. There was a phone call asking if my mother was home. She was not. A while later, right about the time she arrived, some police came to the house. They told her that my dad had a heart attack while on his current construction site. It was his first-ever heart attack and he died that day. No second chance. He was 47. She burst into tears and so did I. I became angry and then eventually settled into a state of numb detachment which lasted a very long time. Peace was nowhere to be found for several years, but not because my dad and I were very close. It was just that I knew no other father and my life, or what I imagined my life to be, was now dismantled and I was incapable of rebuilding it.

It is not the same with the peace of Jesus. At those times when the world's peace is lacking, I have found it helpful to use John 14:27, quoted above, as one of my go-to verses. I will repeat it to myself quietly and thoughtfully and allow it to sink in again and again. And it works. The peace of Christ is far greater than the nagging gap that the world's peace leaves empty. With Christ's peace, there is always more where the first bit came from. It is even more helpful to combine the repetition of that verse with prayer.

Another well-known and well-used passage is found in Phil 4:6-7, "Do not be anxious about anything, but in everything by prayer and supplication with thanksgiving let your requests be made known to God. And the peace of God, which surpasses all understanding, will guard your hearts and your minds in Christ Jesus." I find it helpful to start any given day by taking some of my most troubling thoughts and handing them over to God in prayer. This may contrast with some ideal pictures of a prayer life, where there is joyful worship, intimate communion and then agonizing intercession for the needs of the world. Applause to those whose prayer lives look better than mine. Mine tends to be unpolished. But if you often find your heart troubled and lacking in peace, as I do, usually first thing in the morning and sometimes for weeks or months at a time, I recommend a few well-placed Bible verses combined with prayer. The peace does not usually come instantly, but when a good foundation is laid then that peace can eventually come when you need it most. I think this sort of prayer life and preparation for those special times of need is allowed for in Christ's instructions to his disciples.

For example, take John 16:32-33, "Behold, the hour is coming, indeed it has come, when you will be scattered, each to his own home, and will leave me alone. Yet I am not alone, for the Father is with me. I have said these things to you, that in me you may have peace. In the world you will have tribulation. But take heart; I have overcome the world."

Under the circumstances, at the very moment of Christ's arrest, trial, and crucifixion, it was understandable that the disciples might have found reason to lose their sense of peace or lose heart. Well, or maybe not. Jesus had done his best to prepare them but they, like us, did not always grasp the lesson the first time around, or the second, or, well, you get the point. Therefore, Jesus gives them a final piece of preparation. They are going to be scattered while Jesus is taken, but Christ's betrayal, arrest, and what comes after, are all part of God's plan. Everything is under control. And this is how it is with us as well.

The world is a troubling place, but Jesus knows that. He wants us to remember that he has overcome the world. Will we experience tribulation here in this world? Yes. In fact, it is guaranteed, which must be one of the most dismal promises in the Bible. Nonetheless, Christ has overcome the world and that is a glorious thought, considering how much trouble the world can give us. Think of all the suffering, both just and unjust. Think of the ever-growing number of martyrs, all willingly going to their death, quietly, peacefully, and sometimes joyfully, while never fighting back. Passive martyrdom has always been the Christian ideal. But Jesus has overcome all of that. He has overcome the world.

Let that peace that passes understanding fill your heart and your mind. As it says in Col 3:15, "And let the peace of Christ rule in your hearts, to which indeed you were called in one body. And be thankful." Let Christ take charge of your heart by continuously giving your troubles over to him. He has left us with his peace, but it is one of those things that does not always appear automatically. We need to look for it, wait for it, be ready for it, and above all, take advantage of it and grab hold of it at those times when we need it most. This is what I have found is needed for the personal experience of God's heavenly peace.

An Untroubled Heart

As a reminder, at the beginning and near the end of John 14, in vv. 1 and 27, Jesus says, "Let not your hearts be troubled." We should notice that the "Let not" phrase indicates an imperative, which means Jesus is openly telling us what to do or not do. We are not to let our hearts be troubled. That command should be taken as the instruction of a wise teacher and loving friend, not an order barked by a drill sergeant to a recruit. Underlying the command are some things we may take as the givens, those things that motivate Jesus to issue the command to us. Let's look at them one by one and then suggest a few action steps that will help us work toward an untroubled heart.

First, our hearts may well be inclined to be troubled. If this were not the case, there would be no need for Jesus to tell us to do otherwise. Undeniably, having a troubled heart is an everyday thing for many of us. We should not feel guilty about the mere struggle, but we need to know that giving in to the troubled heart is not a helpful thing. If it were not a common condition, and one to which he could easily foresee his disciples falling prey to in the immediate future, Jesus would likely never have addressed it.

But he mentioned it twice in the same chapter of John. Do not be surprised if you often struggle with a naggingly troubled heart.

Second, an imperative or command tells us that we can do something about this. We are in some measure responsible. We cannot simply say, "That's just how I am," and then conclude that nothing further can be done. The command reminds us that something *can* be done, though what we must do may not be easy. Making changes to our behavior, especially in areas stemming from our internal struggles, is rarely a painless and low-cost endeavor. In fact, such behavior modification can be incredibly difficult. Nor will this change come *naturally.* The very fact that this is an internal, heart-based struggle means that the condition of the troubled heart is probably the most *natural* thing in the world to the one who experiences it. It is a reflex or emotional trigger type of response. Things like this are deeply embedded in our neurology and can be very knotty problems to undo. Nonetheless, they can be undone. This is not Jesus telling a short person to grow taller or vice-versa. It will indeed be difficult and may well seem unnatural, but the command to not let our hearts be troubled is a command that can, in the end, be obeyed. We can make a diligent effort toward obtaining the peace that he promises. With God's help, let us make it a point to be obedient, which brings us to yet another point.

Third, any command to do something requires a response on our part, and that response entails a decision along with some form of conscious effort. This is where we make or break ourselves. We will either live up to the high calling that God has placed upon our lives, or we will not. After a great deal of theological reflection in Chapters 1-3, Paul reminds us in Eph 4:1-3, "I therefore, a prisoner for the Lord, urge you to walk in a manner worthy of the calling to which you have been called, with all humility and gentleness, with patience, bearing with one another in love, eager to maintain the unity of the Spirit in the bond of peace." Decisions, attitudes, effort, and an eagerness to do the right thing – all of this is part of our calling as Christ's followers. To do otherwise will inevitably have dire consequences. C. S. Lewis saw this clearly and explains it well:

I would ... say that every time you make a choice you are turning the central part of you, the part of you that chooses, into something a little different from what it was before. And taking your life as a whole, with all your innumerable choices, all your life long you are slowly turning this central thing either into a heavenly creature or into a hellish creature: either into a creature that is in harmony with God, and with other creatures, and with itself, or else into one that is in a state of war and hatred with God, and with its fellow-creatures, and with itself. To be the one kind of creature is heaven: that is, it is joy and peace and knowledge and power. To be the other means madness, horror, idiocy, rage, impotence, and eternal loneliness. Each of us at each moment is progressing to one state or the other. [12]

This is exactly why each little bit of effort expended toward achieving and maintaining an untroubled heart is worth more than we can know. Our character is being built step by step, one little decision after another. When we give in to what we might call the troubled-heart condition and then stay there, with no effort expended to escape it, we are deciding to remain in what Lewis, just above, calls "a state of war," which is not hyperbole.

The spiritual realm is real and much of what we say and do is connected to it. I say this not to make us nervous, but to make us aware. If we are aware, and we can make a few good decisions in a row, we can get the ball of our brain rolling in the right direction. It then gains momentum, as we all know from either hard or pleasant experience. I have learned that I have to cut off the troubling thoughts early, as in the moment I become aware that they are invading.

We cannot always choose which thoughts will invade our minds. This is one reason we should never despair of our struggles. There are too many factors involved and it might be like

12 C. S. Lewis, C. S., *Mere Christianity*. Kindle Edition. (New York: HarperCollins, 1980), Locations 1162-67

despairing that there is something wrong with us that has caused a particular mugger to try to rob us. Maybe we were the closest potential victim, nothing more. There may of course be ways to make ourselves less of a target for a mugging, for example, through awareness. Similarly, our awareness can make us, over time, less prone to these spiritual thought attacks. But bottom line, neither the mugging nor the thought invasion is our fault. And when that invasion happens, once we know the unproductive thought is there, we can hold on to it or we can immediately try to replace it with something else. Bible verses and short prayers can replace negative or intrusive thoughts.

As for the Bible verses, the two we have already looked at from John 14 are a good place to start. Suppose someone says something or does something, which may or may not be intended to hurt us or set us off, but it does. We feel the emotions rise, the tension increase, and we no longer feel comfortable. If we are aware of our heightened reaction (and it may take some practice to become aware), try to disconnect emotionally from the circumstances and inwardly repeat John 14:1, "Let not your hearts be troubled. Believe in God; believe also in me." Normally I repeat the verse three to ten times. As a prescription I would say "Take as needed." There does not seem to be a predictable number of times to do this on any given day. I would however, even on the best days, do it at least once. It is important to try to calm your body as well as your mind, sometimes with a few deep breaths. It is also important to vary the Bible verse.

After a day, or a few days, or a week, a Bible verse begins to get stale for me. Fresh insights are no longer coming, and the thoughts seem a little routine. At that point I might switch it up. Early in the day I will decide that my new planned verse might be John 14:27, "Peace I leave with you; my peace I give to you. Not as the world gives do I give to you. Let not your hearts be troubled, neither let them be afraid." I will use the verse the same way and the freshness returns. Peace is again more readily available. Then, day by day or week by week, I cycle through any number of Bible verses. The Bible verse habit works quite well, but it is also possible to turn your heart toward God in prayer.

Having go-to prayers is helpful for times like these. They function much as the ready-to-go Bible verses but have the added effect of beginning more of a conversation with God. How we do this may reflect our personalities or taste. Being raised Catholic and beginning my prayer life while still solidly within that tradition, I may not have quite the same aversion to repeating a prayer over and over that some Protestant or Evangelical believers do. Not all repetitions, in my view, are the "vain repetition." Jesus speaks of in Matt 6:7 (KJV). Some can be helpful. One important factor on our end of prayer is the battle to calm and focus our mind. Sure, repetitive prayers can be mindless, but they can also be mindful, especially at the start of a prayer time. Add to all that the fact that many of my spontaneous prayers are inattentive and repetitive, so the line between spontaneous and scripted gets fuzzy very quickly. If you have a problem with a scripted or repeated prayer, then obviously, pray as you wish. I tend to think God wants us to pray so much that he is happy with almost anything that will get us to pray.

One of the little prayers I like to use is more common among Eastern Orthodox or Catholic believers, as are, I suppose, most scripted prayers. This one is loosely based on the prayer of the tax collector in the parable in Luke 18:13, so it is almost like repeating Scripture. The way I like to say it is, "Jesus Christ, Son of God, have mercy on me, the sinner." A little prayer like this can have a wonderfully calming effect when repeated on a regular basis at certain times of the day. This prayer reminds us of our complete dependence upon God and our complete alienation from him due to our sin were it not for his mercy. Again, using it as needed is a helpful tool and a helpful way to reconnect our heart with our Savior.

Another possibility is to use a scripted prayer of your own. For example, since we are on an overall Fatherhood of God theme, one that I might say is, "Father, I thank you that you have made me your son. Help me to honor you, help me to obey you, help me to trust you, help me to love you, and help me to love all my brothers and sisters in Christ. Amen." A prayer like that can help bring me back to a balanced center when I detect that I am losing my balance emotionally. It reminds me who I am (a child of God). It directs me to a proper attitude toward our Father (honor, obedience, trust and love) and a right focus (love) when I think of our brothers and sisters in Christ. Like all prayer, it also reminds us of our complete dependence upon God. No sense fighting spiritual battles with earthly resources. Finally, it is helpful that it is short and easy to remember, since we want to be able to go to it numerous times a day if needed. It is that persistence that I find pays off.

Persistence Is the Key

An untroubled heart is not always easy to come by, and may be harder for some than for others, but it is possible. Like all steps in spiritual growth, we do things with God's help, in his strength, and we must be sure to always keep at it. I can find myself going to these little exercises multiple times per day, and day after day after day. The fact that I must do that may well be the result of genetics or environment, nature or nurture or some combination thereof. I do not know the cause precisely and I do not believe it is what counts most in the end. Different people deal with different things.

What we all face, however, is what amounts to an imperative or direct bit of instruction from Jesus to not let our hearts be troubled. Running amok and all on their own, those hearts of ours might be troubled much more than we know. Therefore, we need to follow Jesus' instructions to not let that be the case.

In those instructions, I find it helpful to break the whole idea down into pieces as we did at the beginning. First, we focus on our relationship with God as Father. It is essential to keep reminding ourselves of this relationship if we expect to grow in our understanding of it. Second, our faith in Jesus as God should be on the same level as our faith in God the Father. Christ's imperatives are God's imperatives. His comfort or peace is God's comfort or peace. Third, we need the personal experience of this God-given heavenly peace. Christ offers it, so we know it must be available, but it will be the outcome of prayer and the consistent self-reminder that God has things perfectly under control. Christ has overcome the world. And fourth, there is an untroubled heart, which is attainable through much practice and persistence. Step back from the troubling thoughts and replace them with the thoughts of God. Use a Scripture verse or short prayer that you can focus on, something that will turn your heart toward God our Father and away from the source of the present trouble.

Once again, be persistent. It is possible that none of the above points will truly help us without this. A fleeting thought about God's Fatherhood will not do it. Repeated meditation on the subject, a reminder of our dependence upon him, will decrease our internal trouble over time. Persistence is strongly associated with God's peace and the reassurance regarding God's character and love toward us. That is what we ultimately need.

We also need to remember that our relationship with God is truly like no other. His Fatherhood is unique. We might say it is *exclusive*, since no one else can be allowed to share the exact relationship with us that we have with him. We will now explore that exclusive relationship in greater detail.

CHAPTER 7
EXCLUSIVE FATHERHOOD

"One father is more than a hundred schoolmasters."
– George Herbert, *Jacula Prudentum [Darts of the Wise]; Or,*
Outlandish Proverbs, Sentences, &C.

In Matt 23:8-10, we read, "But you are not to be called rabbi, for you have one teacher, and you are all brothers. And call no man your father on earth, for you have one Father, who is in heaven. Neither be called instructors, for you have one instructor, the Christ."

We should exercise some caution in trying to take this passage quite literally, because if we do so it would force us into odd contortions of speech that would border on the bizarre. I coordinate the faculty for Horizon University in Indiana, and we use the word *instructor* all the time. No one ever comments on whether that is appropriate among Christians. It would be hard to know what else to call them, since *professor* or *teacher* would seem to fall into the exact same trap. This is, of course, only if in fact it is a trap, but I do not believe that it is.

Our Attitude Toward Human Leaders

What I believe Jesus is driving at here is not so much the use of a word, but an attitude of heart. The function of the "pastors and teachers" defined by Paul in Eph 4:11 is a valid role in the church. God intends certain people to fill the role, he gifts them accordingly, and gives them to the church where he expects them to fulfill their ministry. They, along with other church leaders, are God's appointed means, if you will, "for the equipping of the saints for the work of ministry, for the edifying of the body of Christ" (Eph 4:12). We should not be afraid to use the word "teacher," "instructor" or even "rabbi" depending on the context in its mainly descriptive sense. There is a sense, however, that is more than descriptive.

Jesus speaks to that sense just prior to the verses in focus. Indeed, the verses in focus are his response to the condition that he brings up, which was common enough among the scribes and Pharisees to warrant Christ's attention. The condition is still with us today, as we can see from Matt 23:1-7:

> Then Jesus said to the crowds and to his disciples, "The scribes and the Pharisees sit on Moses' seat, so do and observe whatever they tell you, but not the works they do. For they preach, but do not practice. They tie up heavy burdens, hard to bear, and lay them on people's shoulders, but they themselves are not willing to move them with their finger. They do all their deeds to be seen by others. For they make their phylacteries broad and their fringes long, and they love the place of honor at feasts and the best seats in the synagogues and greetings in the market-places and being called rabbi by others.

The issue then, is not so much the precise title or the word we use to describe the person fulfilling the role. It is the attitude with which one holds the position and the kind of respect one believes is due from others as a result. Jesus is critical of those who do not practice what they preach, those who look down upon others as if they were not held to the same standards, and those who love to receive special honor because of the seat they occupy or the role in which they serve. It is easy here to think of the celebrity pastor, the scholar with the massive ego, or the minister who is capable of working a crowd with an almost cynical political savvy worthy of any prime minister in the secular political realm.

Craig Blomberg captures the gist as well as anyone, wisely pointing out that in our day no church would be immune. "One thinks of modern 'high church' ceremonialism and 'low church' showmanship, both of which often distract from true worship by calling unnecessary attention to the human worship leaders" [13] So much for the instructors or rabbis, but what about the *fathers*? Again, we have to look at the heart.

Using the Title of Father

It is safe to assume the fifth commandment is not somehow blasphemous when it says, "Honor your father and your mother, that your days may be long in the land that the Lord your God is giving you" (Exod 20:12). We should honor our fathers. To label them as such, if that is who they are, cannot be a problem. How else can we define who it is that God expects us to honor? There is also the sense in which the Bible uses the word "fathers" when it is speaking of ancestors or predecessors, particularly in the realm of faith. The Epistle to the Hebrews (Heb 1:1) begins, "Long ago, at many times and in many ways, God spoke to our fathers by the prophets." Yet it is here where we inch closer to Matt 23:9 "And call no man your father on earth."

Blomberg is again helpful when he states, "'Father' was apparently reserved for the patriarchs and revered teachers from the past," and he backs that up by a reference to the Talmud.[14] There is a place where respect oozes into reverence and begins to cross a dangerous line. One can easily imagine the rabbis citing these "Fathers" with an authority and admiration that perhaps should have been reserved for God alone. We do not encounter it so much these days, but we can envision a time or place where the Church

---

13 Blomberg, C. (1992). *Matthew: An Exegetical and Theological Exposition of Holy Scripture*, Kindle edition, New American Commentary (Nashville, TN: B & H Publishing Group, 1992), 342.
14 Ibid

Fathers were held by some with a similar reverence. To cite ancient scholars such as Clement of Rome, Athanasius or Augustine was at one time akin to citing the authoritative interpretation of a matter, near to the word of God itself. But for most of us, outside the most traditional circles of the church, those days are gone.

I suspect the closest thing I am familiar with, which might qualify as a misuse of the word *father* is when it is used of a Catholic priest ("Father Sal" or "Father Kowalski"). Further along the same line would be when one refers to the Pope as "the Holy Father," which is common enough. If I were a priest or a pope, where even the title *pope* seems to derive from some early form of the word *father,* I would have to wonder if this was not a textbook example of the very thing that Jesus is telling us to avoid.

God's Unique Fatherhood

Whatever it is that Jesus wants us guard against, there is a reason that we should avoid it. The reason Jesus gives is that we have one Father, who is in heaven. If God is our Father, then there is a certain type of fatherhood that must be set aside and only thought of when we think of him. We might call it *ultimate* fatherhood or even *exclusive* fatherhood, since no other fatherhood can compare with it. In fact, once we consider the Fatherhood of God, then any other fatherhood, whether biological, metaphorical, or any other kind, is by comparison no real fatherhood at all. Let's consider a few fatherly characteristics.

A reasonable place to start is with that fifth commandment, which says you should, "Honor your father and your mother …" (Exod 20:12). Both parents are, of course, worthy of honor, but it is the father we are thinking about here. It may be true that these days the father needs to be considered more for honor anyway. A quick Google search of "Down with the Patriarchy" (in quotation marks for accuracy) yielded 558,000 results in 0.46 seconds. These included numerous anti-father or anti-male products on Amazon and Etsy. To offer a comparison, I switched the letter "P" out for an "M" to search "Down with the Matriarchy." It produced half as many results and on closer examination, most of the ones near the top, especially among the products for sale, turned out to be pro-feminism items, and thus not actually negative toward women at all.[15] We might have a long discussion about why this happens, but our point here is somewhere else. We mean to examine the commandment and see how it reflects upon the Fatherhood of God.

As we move toward that target, to be fair, this commandment itself would have sounded different in a more traditional society than our own. In the western world, and in the USA perhaps first and foremost, we seem to have done everything we can to systematically destroy every traditional norm or value we can find. This applies to even the most obvious and least harmful, such as giving parents a certain level of honor. A society such as the Near East would likely still believe this commandment seems only right. In the ancient Near East (the time and place where the commandment was given) that would only have been truer than it is today. The culture was *patriarchal* in a way that everyone would have considered healthy. Fatherhood communicated respect, stability, tradition, and strength, whereas the same word, *patriarchal,* now seems in North America to be synonymous with all that is wrong. We should remind ourselves that we have a natural bias. Just like every generation and culture, we tend to assume our way of looking at things must be the more correct. The bias becomes perilous when it seems to contradict the word of God.

We might also take note of the accusation that God brings before the people through the prophet Malachi, "A son honors his father, and a servant his master. If then I am a father, where is my honor? And if I am a master, where is my fear? says the Lord of hosts to you, O priests, who despise my name … (Malachi 1:6). In this historical context the priests were not giving God the honor he was due. If he was in any sense the father of the nation of Israel, then there was a certain honor due him as a result. God shakes the comparison in their faces on the grounds that "A son honors his father." The underlying assumption is that sons typically do honor

---

15 Both searches were done on April 29, 2022.

their fathers, which is normal and right. In this case, however, the people (in particular, the priests) were not bothering to honor God. It is not the point of the passage, but from it we can see that the two forms of honor, to a father and to God, are then firmly and clearly related.

So, if we consider the natural honor due to a father, as the fifth commandment would require, we can also jump up to the first of all commandments, in Exod 20:2-3, "I am the Lord your God, who brought you out of the land of Egypt, out of the house of slavery. You shall have no other gods before [or besides] me." This is an honor, a loyalty, and an exclusiveness that is rightly due to the only true God. God is not only the one true God of Israel but is the only God worthy of the name. If all other beings in heaven or on earth, in the natural or the spiritual realm, are mere creations, then the honor due to the only Creator must be a unique honor indeed.

His fatherhood is also a very unique fatherhood. Again, it is an ultimate fatherhood or an exclusive sort of fatherhood, because no other fatherhood can compare with it on an equal or interchangeable level. Paul sees it clearly in what he says in his letter to the Ephesians.

The Origins of Fatherhood

"For this reason, I bow my knees before the Father, from whom every family in heaven and on earth is named" (Eph 3:14-15). Please excuse a little venture into the original Greek, which can sometimes help. The word for "family" in this section is the Greek *patria.* It is obviously related to word for "Father," used of God just before that, which is *Pater.* Mixing the languages a little, the sentence would sound something like this, "For this reason I bow my knees before the *Pater*, from whom every *patria* in heaven and on earth is named." This is a beautifully clear place to see the absolutely unique or exclusive fatherhood of God. All other fatherhood, every family, whether in heaven or on earth, derives its very name from the original, the prototypical fatherhood of God. If such is the relationship of God to fatherhood, generally speaking, then Jesus makes a perfectly valid point in telling us not to call any man on earth our father because we really do have only one Father, and he is in heaven. Despite the proper honor due to fathers, the fact remains that earthly fatherhood is drawn out of something else. The very concept of a father, who is a father only because there is a family who knows him as such, is a concept that derives from the Fatherhood of God.

From a Fatherless Perspective

In this situation, the fatherless individual might even have a rare and slight advantage over others. In a way, it can be easier to look to our heavenly Father as *Father* when there is no one on earth that automatically fills that role. Importantly, I am saying it can be *easier in a way*. It would be inaccurate to say it is outright *easy*. Fatherlessness tends to create confusion, alienation, mistrust and an enduring chip on one's shoulder, especially in sons. This can be overcome, to be sure, but it often needs special attention. Nonetheless, when one is unsure where to turn to find a father, the fatherhood of God can, with a little effort, become an attractive prospect. God can be there day in and day out, even when there is no one who automatically comes to mind as the right man to honor on Father's Day.

When we need a provider, he is there. When we need a protector, he is there. When we need an example, good advice or good counsel, there he is again. When we need the voice of experience, we have someone who has been around from eternity past and, in fact, has created all there is and knows all there is to know. And unlike those typical human fathers whom we truly ought to honor despite their flaws, this Father has no flaws that we are required to put up with or overlook. There is no real comparison to be made if we try to compare our God to an earthly father. The more we consider his character, his qualities and his attributes, the clearer it should be that he is a Father like no other. The deeper we probe, the better we understand that he deserves the title Father in a way that no human father ever can.

The Best Father of All

We should continuously look to our heavenly Father in ways and at times when we might feel the need to consult with a father figure. Fathers fall short, but this Father will never disappoint. Or better, *if* he seems to disappoint, it is an indication that *our own* attitude needs an adjustment. We may *feel* disappointed but that is due more to our own expectations than any fault in him. Earthly fathers do fall short in wisdom. So much about them simply must be imperfect, even if we have the best father that we could ever hope to have. This father is flawless, complete in every good quality that there is to name. What more could we ask for in a father?

God the Father is the best father of all. We have been adopted into a family in which Christ our Lord is our brother on the human level. Now, with God as our Father, we have the best Father that there is or truly ever shall be. As Jesus valued his relationship with the Father, we can now do the same. It will definitely take practice and it may take hard work, but the attitude that we develop toward our Father should be somehow imitative of the relationship that Christ, while on earth, enjoyed with him. Think of just some of the evidence we see in the Gospels.

The Son and His Father

One of the clearest places this closeness comes out is in Christ's constant desire and determination to be in prayer. In Matt 14:23, just after feeding the 5,000 just prior to walking on water, we see Jesus going off by himself to spend time with his Father. "And after he had dismissed the crowds, he went up on the mountain by himself to pray. When evening came, he was there alone." This sort of thing was a common practice for him. Mark records the same type of thing in Mark 1:35, "And rising very early in the morning, while it was still dark, he departed and went out to a desolate place, and there he prayed." Luke goes a step farther contrasting the gathering crowds with the habit Jesus had of getting alone so he could pray, "But now even more the report about him went abroad, and great crowds gathered to hear him and to be healed of their infirmities. But he would withdraw to desolate places and pray." (Luke 5:15-16) How different Jesus is in this regard from me.

While I do pray regularly, even daily and often many times a day, I still do not see within myself that special something that I would describe as a spontaneous, deeply held desire for that kind of fellowship with my Father. I do not see it in the way I see it in Jesus, at any rate. He seems to have gone way out of his way to make sure he had sufficient time in prayer, sufficient time with his Father. In Christ's case, I do not believe this was a matter of sticking to a routine or something done out of exceptional self-discipline. He knew that he needed exactly this sort of time and made sure that the time was carved out and well spent. I do not do that enough and it is probably because I do not quite value it enough. I do not perceive the need or sense the desire to spend time with my Father in the same way that Jesus did. Those two, Jesus and his Father, were connected in ways that we can only imagine from our end.

Take the brief and simple, yet marvelously profound statement, "I and the Father are one" (John 10:30). It is no doubt beyond anything we can grasp to fathom the depths of what this statement means to its fullest extent. And yet, at the same time, there is something in it that Jesus wanted for all of us. Before he departed, he prayed for that to be true. "And I am no longer in the world, but they are in the world, and I am coming to you. Holy Father, keep them in your name, which you have given me, that they may be one, even as we are one" (John 17:11). He prayed further, "O righteous Father, even though the world does not know you, I know you, and these know that you have sent me. I made known to them your name, and I will continue to make it known, that the love with which you have loved me may be in them, and I in them." Thoughts like these, I am convinced, relate to this exclusive level of Fatherhood that we ought to experience toward God.

Our Use of Titles

There is a unity of the Father and the Son that is not shared by anyone else, but Christ still desires that we somehow share it with one another. Beyond that, Christ has made the Father known to us, and will continue to do so. We need to know this love. We need to take the perspective that God is our Father. Some of the ways we use titles or respect persons here on earth may not be appropriate in the end. Our use of Reverend, Pastor, Doctor, Professor or Rabbi, etc. may cross a line. If we desire to hear such titles from others, it is more likely that a line has been crossed. In the realm of God's Fatherhood, however, it only makes sense to listen to the advice this older brother of ours gives. "And call no man your father on earth, for you have one Father, who is in heaven." He is the only Father that we can all share and that we will ever need.

Having seen God as our exclusive Father, we are ready to look at two important fatherly characteristics that are especially his. In the next two chapters we will contemplate God as our Provider and then as our Protector.

CHAPTER 8
THE FATHER AS PROVIDER

"The child asks of the Father whom he knows. Thus, the essence of Christian prayer is not general adoration, but definite, concrete petition. The right way to approach God is to stretch out our hands and ask of One who we know has the heart of a Father."
— Dietrich Bonhoeffer, *The Cost of Discipleship*

Most of us are familiar with the request in Christ's model prayer which says, "Give us this day our daily bread" (Matt 6:11). And most of us who pray at all probably understand that God knows our needs. Even earthly fathers can do a pretty good job of knowing what their children need, whether they ask or not, and many times know better than the children themselves. More on that in a little bit.

Still Jesus tells us to ask. This request for daily bread, which is embedded in Christ's instruction on prayer, points us in the direction of God as the most fundamental Provider of all our most basic requirements. We were never intended to be self-sufficient beings. God clearly conveyed this idea to the Israelites back in Deuteronomy before they entered the Promised Land:

> Take care lest you forget the Lord your God by not keeping his commandments and his rules and his statutes, which I command you today, lest, when you have eaten

and are full and have built good houses and live in them, and when your herds and flocks multiply and your silver and gold is multiplied and all that you have is multiplied, then your heart be lifted up, and you forget the Lord your God, who brought you out of the land of Egypt, out of the house of slavery, ... Beware lest you say in your heart, "My power and the might of my hand have gotten me this wealth." You shall remember the Lord your God, for it is he who gives you power to get wealth, that he may confirm his covenant that he swore to your fathers, as it is this day.

If we consider the context, we can easily understand that the Israelites were going to have to farm the land and raise their own flocks to access this God-given provision. They knew that, too. God was not intending to do anything obviously supernatural for them in Canaan as he did in the desert of Sinai by providing them with manna day by day. Consequently, the risk in their new environment, where work and planning, planting and harvesting would all bring about consistent and reliable results, is that the people would only see what they did for themselves and no longer see God's hand in it. When you work hard for a living, it is not nearly as noticeable that God is at work in your own efforts. We may admire the *self-made* man but there are no self-made men in God's world.

Keeping God in Mind

No matter how hard we try, our own power, hard work and creative ideas will get us only so far. Or better, they will never accomplish anything of value unless God is busily working behind the scenes. Without him, we are building windmills, but still waiting around for some wind. We are building a better mousetrap in a place where there are no mice. We are planting acorns in the desert where oak trees cannot grow. The Lord our God gives us the power to get wealth. He is our ultimate Provider, the one who provides the means that we use to achieve the desired ends. This is likely one reason he asks us to pray about our needs.

When we ask God for daily bread, we do not expect manna from heaven, but we may need a job. If we have a job, we must never expect that job security or success in our endeavors is something we can simply assume. Hard-working people go broke when their opportunities dry up and disappear. Companies that were once massive generators of wealth for their owners and employees can go out of business when the markets shift, or some new technology comes along to replace the old one to which they were committed. Any prayer for provision, for "our daily bread," can be thought of as a prayer that our work will be effective and that it would be the channel through which God the Father provides for our needs. He gives us the power to get wealth and we can count on him.

Two Extreme Personal Examples

As a young man and a new Christian, I decided to put God to the test in getting a job. This was a low-risk test because I had just finished high school and was living at home with my mother. In the summer, I had previously worked for both the town Parks and Recreation Departments but this year, exuberant with faith, I decided not to turn in an application. I would instead trust God to provide. The day that summer employment for the town would start was drawing near and I still had no job or any means of making money. Things were getting tense at home since my mother did not share my faith or my immaturity. Perhaps prompted by my mother, or simply not seeing me on the list of summer hires, my uncle, who worked for the town himself, gave me a call. He asked if I had applied for a job, and I said no. If he asked why not I certainly did not give a convincing answer. Normally impatient, he now became audibly upset. Within an hour or so, he met me at a designated place, job application in hand. He stood over me fuming while I awkwardly filled it out using his car as a desktop. Within a few days I got a call to start work for the town at minimum wage and the job would last all summer. God had indeed provided but if you put him too much to the test, it may make your uncle mad. I concluded it was unwise to use that method of finding work again, though uncles can do only so much.

The second story goes in the opposite direction. Years later, after completing college debt free, thanks to considerable financial aid from both the federal government and the state of New York, I was now planning to move to San Diego to join a friend. Having both an AAS in Electrical Engineering Technology and a BA in Music, I was now at least a little more qualified for something. Figuring the electrical degree was more useful for employment, and these being pre-internet days, I spent chilly evenings downtown in the Buffalo Public Library, where I pulled out the San Diego phone book and found addresses for prospective employers. I sent over 100 resumes to companies that sounded like they employed electrical or electronics types. When I finally got to San Diego, I had a grand total of one interview for my efforts. Trying to look and act my best, I went to the designated office and was promptly told by the interviewer that he was unsure why I was there. They had no positions open for anyone remotely like me. Goodbye and good luck. And so began the long process of knocking on doors, turning in resumes, and filling out applications. At least it was warmer and sometimes sunny.

Looking for work eight hours a day and prayerfully deciding never to say no to a possible paycheck, it still took months before I got a job that would last. I delivered furniture, helped assembling video games (which was clearly the most fun) and moved heavy boxes around in an auto parts warehouse. But in the end, all these places laid me off when the need for my efforts died down. I was back on the streets stressfully praying, eating very cheaply, and looking for employment. Eventually it came, in the form of calibration and quality control of electronic instruments. The process of finding a job this time around seemed completely non-supernatural. God was in it, of course, but the inward feeling was that it was very much up to me.

Christ's Teaching on God's Provision

In an extensive passage within the Sermon on the Mount, Jesus teaches us not to worry about whether the Father will provide for our needs:

> Therefore I tell you, do not be anxious about your life, what you will eat or what you will drink, nor about your body, what you will put on. Is not life more than food, and the body more than clothing? Look at the birds of the air: they neither sow nor reap nor gather into barns, and yet your heavenly Father feeds them. Are you not of more value than they? And which of you by being anxious can add a single hour to his span of life? And why are you anxious about clothing? Consider the lilies of the field, how they grow: they neither toil nor spin, yet I tell you, even Solomon in all his glory was not arrayed like one of these. But if God so clothes the grass of the field, which today is alive and tomorrow is thrown into the oven, will he not much more clothe you, O you of little faith? Therefore, do not be anxious, saying, "What shall we eat?" or "What shall we drink?" or "What shall we wear?" For the Gentiles seek after all these things, and your heavenly Father knows that you need them all. But seek first the kingdom of God and his righteousness, and all these things will be added to you. (Matt 6:25-33)

How much time and energy do we spend worrying about the very things Jesus talks about here in this passage? If I answer the question honestly for myself, it would be embarrassing to see the accumulated total time. I might make excuses, perhaps pointing back to the fatherless condition that may have acted as a catalyst to worry. That condition may have given rise to a feeling that the world was stacked against me and that I needed to fight for any little advantage I could get. No one wants to be left helpless and hopeless once and for all. But in this passage, Jesus does not seem to be leaving us much room for excuses.

Jesus is not asking us why we might worry but teaching why we should trust. His point is that we ought to look to our Father in heaven as our Provider. Christ knows better than anyone that there may be reasons, causes or catalysts to our worried state. Since Joseph disappears early from the Gospels, Jesus the young man may well have been left without his father while still fairly young, causing him to be the family's main provider before he had fully come of age. Reasons, however, are not quite the same thing as excuses. Jesus' goal is that we should not be anxious.

After we add up all the reasons why we may be overly concerned about providing for ourselves, Jesus responds with "Do not be anxious." It is his message to our worried condition. He sees our needs, he sees all the factors that play into our anxiety, and he responds with "Look at the birds of the air: they neither sow nor reap nor gather into barns, and yet your heavenly Father feeds them. Are you not of more value than they?"

If we understood our relationship to our Father in heaven, our worries would rapidly begin to wither and die. There is no need to worry when you know beyond a shadow of a doubt that your Father knows what you lack, your Father cares, and your Father has the power, resources and desire to take care of you. And Jesus takes it further than that:

> And why are you anxious about clothing? Consider the lilies of the field, how they grow: they neither toil nor spin, yet I tell you, even Solomon in all his glory was not arrayed like one of these. But if God so clothes the grass of the field, which today is alive and tomorrow is thrown into the oven, will he not much more clothe you, O you of little faith? (Matt 6:28-30)

A Father who pays that much attention to clothing the lilies of the field and sees to it that they are clothed better than Solomon can certainly take care of you and me. He will give me clothing to stay warm in winter and to make myself presentable when I have to go out in public. He cares for me, and if he has so much that he is able to make the grass beautiful and still let it wither so quickly, then he must also have enough on hand to supply all of our necessities. My responsibility is to make sure that I am placing my trust in him rather than worrying about how to provide for myself. I need to be diligent to attend to the tasks he places before me, but I must do so without imagining that I am my own provider.

Sound Advice from the Proverbs and Colossians

A few verses from Proverbs drive this point home with the emphasis on our being willing to work hard at whatever God calls us to do.

The first is Proverbs 10:4, "A slack hand causes poverty, but the hand of the diligent makes rich." This verse clearly connects hard work with financial gain. If we expect God to provide for us, then doing the work he assigns to us is the most important step we can take to seeing his provision for our needs.

The next example is Proverbs 13:4, "The soul of the sluggard craves and gets nothing, while the soul of the diligent is richly supplied." There is blessing in diligence, and it is the normal way that God provides for us. The term sluggard is not complementary. The character of the lazy man is rightly called into question, while the diligent person is expressing a godly virtue as their work gets done.

Another verse with similar insight is Proverbs 14:3, "In all toil there is profit, but mere talk tends only to poverty." This is a blunt reminder that making empty promises or boasting about what we are going to do is a pointless exercise. Getting to work is more important than talking about what we hope to accomplish.

A great New Testament passage to keep in mind is Colossians 3:23-24, "Whatever you do, work heartily, as for the Lord and not for men, knowing that from the Lord you will receive the inheritance as your reward. You are serving the Lord Christ." Our hard work is a way of serving Jesus. We take care to do the work assigned to us and God takes care of our needs. The real beauty here is that the "inheritance" we receive as a "reward" speaks of our future reward in eternity. In other words, we can store up treasure in heaven by doing our job well on earth. That is a wonderful encouragement at times when the earthly reward seems a bit less than we hoped.

Learning to Ask

When we combine a willingness to work hard with a quiet trust in what God has promised, we get a firmer grasp on God as both Father and Provider. We serve him when we work hard, work ethically, and seek to serve him in all that we do. And yet, in the end, he always remains the one who gives us all that we need. We do not provide for ourselves.

As his children, we do not really work for our provision. We work to be faithful, to be diligent and to be obedient in what our Father calls us to do. The provision part is up to him. This is a tremendous relief during especially lean times or any other time of uncertainty – and such times can come fairly often whether we are prone to worrying about our needs or not. As we cultivate a childlike trust, we should look to him expectantly as the source of all that we shall ever have.

Very early on in our time in Poland, shortly after communism fell, my wife Ginger and I had arranged for some financial support to be sent our way. Unfortunately, the banking system was still lagging behind European standards. The fact that I had received some financial support in the Netherlands for several years was irrelevant since the banks in Poland were still operating in a cold war, iron curtain environment. We had money in the bank in California but were running out of money in Poland and were not yet getting paid for teaching. What could we do?

We prayed a lot and accepted some invitations for meals, which our hospitable new Polish friends regularly offered. On a Saturday morning when we were down to about twenty-five cents American, there was a knock at the door. It was the mailman, who didn't usually come on Saturday, and he had an envelope we needed to sign for from our Dutch bank. It was a check for about $100 US, but in Dutch Gulden (pre-Euro days). The bank decided they didn't want such a small account with a Polish name and address so they closed it without us asking and sent us the money. On Sunday, we accepted one of those free Polish dinners from a friend who didn't know we had no cash or food left in the cupboard. As Americans, we felt kind of embarrassed to admit that. On Monday, I took the check to our Polish bank and found out that bank checks would immediately be turned into cash. On the way home, I stopped at the grocery store and our dinner that day, thanks to God's obvious provision, was the best we had tasted in a long time.

No child should ever have to worry about where their next meal or their necessary clothing is going to come from. Most children quickly learn that all they have to do is ask. They may not get all that they ask for, but their parents surely try to give them all that they need – including those things which they ask for that are good. That brings us to another of the teachings of Jesus, which combines lessons on provision and prayer:

> Ask, and it will be given to you; seek, and you will find; knock, and it will be opened to you. For everyone who asks receives, and the one who seeks finds, and to the one who knocks it will be opened. Or which one of you, if his son asks him for bread, will give him a stone? Or if he asks for a fish, will give him a serpent? If you then, who are evil, know how to give good gifts to your children, how much more will your Father who is in heaven give good things to those who ask him! (Matt 7:7-11)

There is probably no better passage to meditate on in order to cultivate a childlike faith and trust in our Father's willingness to meet all of our needs. It all begins with our learning to ask. I strongly suspect there is something going on here from God's side, which he knows the act of *asking* will teach us. He knows our needs, but still reserves the right to wait for his children to ask, seek, and knock. It may be that he likes us to retain some helpful sense of independence even as we depend upon him. When we come to him willingly with our requests, we do it as a sort of personal choice, even if the needs themselves are not needs of our own choosing. A person who chooses *not* to pray when confronted with needs would be illustrating a lack of faith or trust in our heavenly Father. They may look to merely human methods or earthly resources instead. At the same time, this very asking, the very presenting of our requests, reminds us of our dependence upon God for all of our basic provision. There are wonderful lessons to be learned in this back and forth aspect of the relationship as he teaches us to rely upon him.

Valuable Lessons Learned in Prayer

The very asking requires a kind of discipline. Day after day, we come to our Father because we are confronted with the fact that it seems that we always need something. The needs themselves are used by God to encourage a prayerful relationship. If these needs were always met without our ever asking, we might easily forget that prayer was a necessary part of our spiritual growth. God allows us to have various needs, at least in part, so that we have some motivation to come to him in prayer. And while we are there, we learn a few valuable lessons. For example:

1. We learn the necessity of prayer.
2. We learn the value of prayerful activity.
3. We learn something about the character of God.

And no doubt even more, but let's consider first *the necessity of prayer*. There is probably no Christian, or at least no Christian with any credibility, that would argue *against* our need for prayer. We already know it to be true. We frequently feel it. We are sometimes aware of it as a vague sense of guilt or inadequacy that we need to pray and never pray enough. While this may make us feel like less-than-ideal Christians, we probably know very few Christians who are convinced that their prayer lives fully measure up. This discrepancy between theory and practice, between attitudes and actions, is a curious thing. We know that we should pray and yet we also know that we do not pray as we ought. We may not be able to solve that problem all at once here and now, but we can observe something important related to God. To help us in our prayer life, he cultivates within us a healthy sense of dependence. He fosters dependence as he allows us to experience need.

When we have needs, and we usually do have them, we can take these as cues from a loving heavenly Father. He is continuously working by means of the intricacies of providence, allowing our circumstances to stay somewhere beyond our control. The bills that always need to be paid, the friendships that need our responsiveness and the many situations that often leave us wondering what to do – these are ultimately governed by his grace. The Father uses all of these as tools to get our attention despite the natural resistance of our fallen nature and the overall fallen condition of this fallen world. Sin has complicated everything around us, but our perceived needs remind us most of all of our overriding need for him. And this need should prompt us to pray. Prayer is more valuable to our spiritual life than we usually acknowledge, and probably more valuable than we can ever know. But we do not *only* pray.

We learn the *value of prayerful activity*. Every time we pray and no matter how much we pray, life will still just keep going. We come out of our prayer closet, arise from our knees, or get up out of that favorite *prayer chair* only to dive back into that daily grind. In so doing, we should always remain conscious of the prayers we have been prompted to offer.

While we cannot make God answer our prayers or *do* anything that would oblige him to give us an answer, we may have to look for those opportunities that signal to us an answer to prayer. As we "watch and pray" that we may not "enter into temptation" (Matt 26:41), we are many times watching for answers to prayer. An offer may present itself; a phone call may come from our uncle. We may see some form of open door placed before us, or the mailman may knock on our door. This is how God normally works. The *ask, seek* and *knock,* that Jesus refers to seem to refer to more than just prayer. They point to the activity we need to engage in while watching and waiting for answers. All of this watching, waiting, praying and, according to God's perfect time-table and perfect will, seeing our prayers answered, also teaches us valuable lessons about God's nature or personality.

We learn *something about the character of God.* When God moves in answer to prayer, he will act only in accordance with his will. The Apostle John tells us, "And this is the confidence that we have toward him, that if we ask anything according to his will he hears us. And if we know that he hears us in whatever we ask, we know that we have the requests that we have asked of him." If we keep our prayers consistent with God's revealed will, we can persistently pray with confidence that our heavenly Father will ultimately answer our cries. As Tony Evans words it, commenting on Matt 7:7-8, "Prayer is an earthly request for heavenly intervention. It doesn't make God do what's outside his will but releases him to do what is inside his will. God has determined that he will not do certain things until asked." [16] Our asking, then, is one way to participate in fulfilling the will of God. He allows us to be confronted with needs we cannot meet so that we cry out to our Father who can be trusted in our time of need. He then answers in accordance with his will, and we learn something of what he is like. We get to know him more personally and begin to better understand his character. But what if we are unsure of God's will?

Learning the Will of the Father

Sometimes we do not know the will of God because we are unfamiliar with the word of God, but that is not always the case. For example, the Bible itself may not be perfectly clear on the topic. Seldom will we find guidance on which job offer to take

16 Tony Evans, *The Tony Evans Bible Commentary* (Nashville: B & H Publishing Group, 2019), Matthew 7

or which house to live in from the Bible. In such cases, it is always best to keep praying, along with engaging in some of that above-mentioned prayerful activity, because persistence in prayer is clearly taught by Jesus. (See Luke 18.) If, on the other hand, our prayers are inconsistent with the will of God, then he simply will answer with a no.

James adds to the conversation from this other side saying, "You ask and do not receive, because you ask wrongly, to spend it on your passions" (James 4:3). Now surely there are times when people pray incorrectly. Perhaps these are individuals who do not really know God, do not relish his word, or are simply immature believers in Christ. For the first two categories, the issue is critical and big changes need to take place in their hearts. For the third group, the immature believers, there is still much hope, and at some level most of us probably fit into this group. We are children who have a Father who provides and teaches us at the same time.

It is a common scenario. The kids want one thing, but they do not realize that it will do them more harm than good. They are children and so they cannot see the full effect of what they want. Their father knows better and therefore does not give them what they ask. He answers according to what is best rather than their less informed whims and fleeting fancies. This is near the very core of what it means to have a Father who provides for our needs. This is what it is to have a *Father* rather than a genie who appears and grants wishes whenever we rub the bottle. Prayer is necessary and prayerful activity is perhaps more necessary still. But most needed of all are the lessons we learn through prayer and its answers, non-answers, and delayed answers. This combination of responses teaches us the most about the character of God.

As we grow, mature, and come to know God better, the idea of the Father as Provider will become second nature. At least that is what I am counting on; I am not there yet. But I can foresee a day when trust for his provision will be a way of life, rather than an intentional act on my part. We see it in numerous places in Scripture and it cannot hurt to look at a few to drive this lesson home. Let's start with David in the Psalms.

Trusting God as Provider

The ever-popular Psalm 23 begins with the words, "The Lord is my shepherd; I shall not want." As a responsible shepherd takes care of his sheep, so God gives us what we need. We shall never be lacking. If a shepherd can take care of his sheep to provide for them, how much more shall God provide for us as a Father for his children! It makes me feel irresponsible to doubt. And there is still more to be gleaned from the Psalms:

> Another example is in Psalm 107:8-9, where we read,
> Let them thank the LORD for his steadfast love,
> for his wondrous works to the children of man!
> For he satisfies the longing soul,
> and the hungry soul he fills with good things.

The psalmist here describes an attitude of heart that we can always cultivate. When we think about all that God has done for us, when we actively seek examples of his provision upon which to focus our spiritual vision, then the result should be a more thankful heart. As we thank him, we become more constantly aware of all that he does. He satisfies our longings. He fills our hungry souls with good things. In the end, we may habitually see the good things that he gives, just as James, the Lord's brother was able to see.

I am reminded of James 1:16-17, "Do not be deceived, my beloved brothers. Every good gift and every perfect gift is from above, coming down from the Father of lights, with whom there is no variation or shadow due to change." For the fatherless individual who is unaccustomed to the reliable provision of a father, and anyone else who is tempted not to trust our Father God, this brief passage is packed with help for a troubled heart.

First, James begins by reminding us not to be deceived. An introduction like this implies that in what he is about to say there is going to be ample room for deception. We may not believe what he tells us, or even if we do in theory, in practice our real-life thoughts and actions may illustrate or expose our doubt. Who has never doubted God's provision? Or questioned his willingness, if not his ability, to provide? Such thoughts are mere lies, and we are deceived if we give in to them.

Next, "Every good gift and every perfect gift is from above, coming down from the Father." Where else can we go? If something is good, it comes from God whose very nature is goodness itself. In 1 Chron 16:34, David praised God singing, "Oh give thanks to the Lord, for he is good; for his steadfast love endures forever!" When Solomon had the ark brought into the temple, into the Most Holy Place, "it was the duty of the trumpeters and singers to make themselves heard in unison in praise and thanksgiving to the Lord), and when the song was raised, with trumpets and cymbals and other musical instruments, in praise to the Lord: "For he is good, for his steadfast love endures forever." (2 Chron 5:13).

When Ezra returned to Jerusalem with the captives, they laid the foundation for the rebuilt temple, "And they sang responsively, praising and giving thanks to the Lord, "For he is good, for his steadfast love endures forever toward Israel." (Ezra 3:11)

And because God is so good, he gives good things. In fact, Jesus makes the point rather strongly by comparing God to us in Matt 7:11, "If you then, who are evil, know how to give good gifts to your children, how much more will your Father who is in heaven give good things to those who ask him!"

God as the Source of All That Is Good

Our problem may be, as immature children, that we do not really grasp what is good and what is evil. Therefore, Paul encourages us, "Do not be conformed to this world, but be transformed by the renewal of your mind, that by testing you may discern what is the will of God, what is good and acceptable and perfect" (Rom 12:2). Yet there is hope that we will grow to appreciate the good things that God gives, for in Heb 5:14 the author tells us, "But solid food is for the mature, for those who have their powers of discernment trained by constant practice to distinguish good from evil." We can get there, and when we do, we will be confident that God our Father will give us good things.

James also refers to God as "the Father of lights." Personally, I am not especially sure I know what that means, but I am reminded of what John says in 1 John 1:5-6, "This is the message we have heard from him and proclaim to you, that God is light, and in him is no darkness at all. If we say we have fellowship with him while we walk in darkness, we lie and do not practice the truth." This ties in with James's concern that we might be deceived. If we think God is somehow against us and we are tempted to doubt his love or willingness to give us that which is good, then we are dangerously close to walking in darkness at that point. God is light, he is the Father of lights, and he gives good things to his children.

Finally, James reminds us of God's inability to change. With him, "there is no variation or shadow due to change." When you are perfect in every way, there is no need to ever become anything else. Theologians call this God's *immutability*. There is never any such thing as a change or *mutation* with God. He will never be different. As a result of possessing this attribute, God is reliable in every way at every time, and this will always be the case. The psalmist expressed this lesson in Psalm 102:25-28:

> Of old you laid the foundation of the earth,
> and the heavens are the work of your hands.
> They will perish, but you will remain;
> they will all wear out like a garment.
> You will change them like a robe, and they will pass away,
> but you are the same, and your years have no end.
> The children of your servants shall dwell secure;
> their offspring shall be established before you.

This is the God who accepts us as his children. We no longer must claw our way through the challenges of this world or fight like a feral cat to see to it that we will get our fair share. We can ask him for our daily bread. We can turn to him with our every need. He will always be faithful and will always see to our provision from his abundant supply. He will not always give us exactly what we want or what we ask for because he is our Father, not our slave. We should learn to be like him because he is good, and he gives us good things. In fact, he is the source of all goodness, so all that is good ultimately comes from him. And he is unchanging, so he is perfectly reliable, and this will always be the case.

Learning to trust God our Father as our Provider is an important lesson. Another fatherly trait that he possesses is that of Protector. We will now look at God as our Father and in that role.

CHAPTER 9
THE FATHER AS PROTECTOR

"A mighty fortress is our God,
A bulwark never failing:
Our helper He, amid the flood
Of mortal ills prevailing.
For still our ancient foe
Doth seek to work his woe;
His craft and power are great,
And armed with cruel hate,
On earth is not his equal."
– Martin Luther, translation by Frederick Henry Hedge

Closely related to God the Father's provision is his protection. As Luther's hymn indicates, the world is a cruel place, full of hazards and enemies. Sometimes these are obvious or brazen but often they are concealed, so that only one with the perception granted by wisdom and experience can point them out. No child should ever be left helpless and exposed without someone to defend her. This is a feeling that I have dealt with for as long as I remember. When I feel unsafe, I can lash out at my perceived assailant. Part of me, somewhere deep down, is always ready to fight, usually with words, but occasionally with something more solid. I can give you an example.

One evening we were doing a church event and I was attending the grill, flipping burgers and turning brats to help feed a hungry crowd. A lady who was both a church member and friend came up behind me and started hitting me with a sock (yes *sock,* not *sack*) full of flour. There was no real reason for it. It was an innocent bit of kidding around. The danger level was exactly zero but I was caught off guard. Before I knew what I was doing, I spun around and began hitting the hand holding the soft fabric weapon with the metal tongs I was using on the grill. I may or may not have drawn blood. Within seconds, I, the pastor of the church, attacked my attacker, came to my senses, and apologized profusely. I kept apologizing into the next day.

Such are the responses of my own rodent or lizard-like brain, which pour forth from those neurological levels beneath a more carefully observed reality. Such automatic reactions, both yours and mine, can be overcome and must be controlled. There is a reason, however, for their existence, which in many cases can be traced back to continual, early encountered feelings that you are unsafe. The unprotected child experiences feelings exactly like these and that means a different, fuller account of reality must be learned so that we can consistently overcome those feelings.

Consider a girl who suffers sexual abuse from a father or stepfather. Or imagine the boy who gets nervous about dad coming home because he knows his father will come home drunk and is then often violent and angry. Finally, as our book's main focus, what about children or young adults who simply have no father in the picture? Can anyone really blame them when they struggle to turn to God in a time of trouble when the main thing they feel is abandoned or alone?

God's Protective Heart

In the Bible, we learn of a very different story. As far back as Gen 4:14-15, we find the Lord God promising to somehow defend Cain, of all people, the author of the first recorded human cruelty. After receiving his sentence of perpetual outlaw status for the killing of his brother Abel, Cain answers God saying, "'Behold, you have driven me today away from the ground, and from your face I shall be hidden. I shall be a fugitive and a wanderer on the earth, and whoever finds me will kill me.' Then the LORD said to him, 'Not so! If anyone kills Cain, vengeance shall be taken on him sevenfold.' And the LORD put a mark on Cain, lest any who found him should attack him."

This passage is not a simple one. Exactly what "sevenfold" vengeance would mean against someone who killed another, I am not quite sure. Even harder to understand is what difference that would make to Cain after he is dead. Nor can I explain a "mark" designed to prevent a prospective attacker from killing Cain. Still, the fact that the Lord begins with "Not so!" and the overall impression that God is interested in keeping Cain un-harmed is meaningful and related to our understanding of God as our Protector. It is even more notable because this is Cain we are talking about, Cain the murderer, Cain the prototype of sinful human rebellion. It is easier to understand God promising to pro-tect Abraham.

In Genesis 15:1, to begin one of the main passages in which we find God's covenant with Abraham (or Abram) introduced, it says, "After these things the word of the Lord came to Abram in a vision: 'Fear not, Abram, I am your shield; your reward shall be very great.'" The shield is a defensive weapon. You do not throw a shield like a frisbee in the hope of hitting your enemy in the head. The shield assumes an offensive weapon is coming toward you and that you need something to protect yourself. God will be Abraham's shield.

To have a shield that is conscious, aware, and powerful, in fact, all-knowing and all-powerful, is a comfort nearly beyond words. Abraham had a shield that was looking out for him to pro-tect him. It was a shield whose vision penetrated the strategies of Abraham's enemies while the strategies were still being formed. There was no enemy stronger than Abraham's shield, and this same promise extended to Abraham's descendants.

By the time we get to the end of Deuteronomy, we find Moses proclaiming a blessing over the children of Israel, a blessing that includes,

The eternal God is your dwelling place:
and underneath are the everlasting arms.
And he thrust out the enemy before you
and said, 'Destroy.'
So Israel lived in safety,
Jacob lived alone,
in a land of grain and wine,
whose heavens drop down dew.
Happy are you, O Israel! Who is like you,
a people saved by the Lord,
the shield of your help,
and the sword of your triumph! (Deut 33:27-29)

The safety and prosperity of Israel are clearly high on God's list of priorities. This is not a general statement dealing with platitudes such as, "God loves everyone in the whole wide world." These are specific blessings pronounced upon a specific people. The enemies were real. The protection would be real as well. Throughout their difficult history, enemies have neither decreased in number nor determination to see Israel destroyed. And yet the nation survives with a great measure of prosperity. This is valuable evidence of God's protection on a national level, much like the blessing that Moses prophesied. God also provided for the protection of the individual.

Cities of Refuge

One fascinating way we see God's protection offered is through the cities of refuge. If we turn to Numbers 35, we read:

> And the Lord spoke to Moses, saying, "Speak to the people of Israel and say to them, When you cross the Jordan into the land of Canaan, then you shall select cities to be cities of refuge for you, that the manslayer who kills any person without intent may flee there. The cities shall be for you a refuge from the avenger, that the manslayer may not die until he stands before the congregation for judg-

ment. And the cities that you give shall be your six cities of refuge. You shall give three cities beyond the Jordan, and three cities in the land of Canaan, to be cities of refuge. These six cities shall be for refuge for the people of Israel, and for the stranger and for the sojourner among them, that anyone who kills any person without intent may flee there (Num 35:9-15).

In our place and time, the whole reason for cities of refuge might be difficult to absorb. We have to put ourselves back into that earlier situation. Imagine being part of a tribal society that has never had its own written laws until now, having lived for centuries under the laws of Egypt. This people had no organized political system, at least not until Moses organized the chiefs of the people into heads of thousands, hundreds, fifties, and tens in Exodus 18. Now, however, they were about to, for the first time ever, enter their own land – the land promised to their ancestor Abraham. Life was going to change. Their natural sense of justice had to be channeled into an orderly judicial system. One of the top concerns would be how to handle murder and how to differentiate it from an accidental death.

Under the rubric of life for life, an eye for an eye, a tooth for a tooth, etc., the punishment had to fit the crime. A person might have their hand cut off if they cut off another's hand, but it would not be cut off for stealing. Stealing would require the loss of property. If a man was guilty of murder, that is, of intentionally taking another's life, justice would demand that the perpetrator forfeit his own life as punishment. Such a punishment is, by nature, irreversible. Something more than vigilante justice is needed to ensure that such an extreme punishment is truly required. Enter the concept of the city of refuge.

If a man killed another by accident, this would not be the same thing as murder, but it might very well look like murder to the victim's close relatives. They just lost their brother, father, cousin, or son. To escape the angry, grieving relative who is out to avenge his brother's death, the manslayer could flee to the nearest city of refuge and arrive there before word ever got back to the family of the victim that their relative just died. At this point, the text of Numbers continues, illustrating that a fair trial should be carried out by the congregation to determine if the death was intentional. If it really was an accident, the manslayer was allowed to live. If he was lying about the cause of the victim's death and really did intend to kill him, and there were witnesses, then he would be treated as a murderer. The close relative, otherwise known as the avenger of blood, was to act as the executioner. There was no opportunity to plea bargain and no court of appeals.

Numbers 35:30-31 goes on, "If anyone kills a person, the murderer shall be put to death on the evidence of witnesses. But no person shall be put to death on the testimony of one witness. Moreover, you shall accept no ransom for the life of a murderer, who is guilty of death, but he shall be put to death." The convicted murderer faced certain death, the innocent man was allowed to live by escaping to the city of refuge, and no rich criminal was allowed to buy off the court. This combination of outcomes sheds a little light on these verses from Proverbs:

> The name of the Lord is a strong tower;
> the righteous man runs into it and is safe.
> A rich man's wealth is his strong city,
> and like a high wall in his imagination. (Prov 18:10-11)

What the city of refuge was to the innocent manslayer, the Lord is to the righteous, who run to him for protection. Wealth, by contrast, which the world often thinks of as the bottom line when it comes to security, offers only imaginary safety. God devised just laws for the newly forming nation of Israel, so that criminals would face justice while the one who was accused but acquitted could remain free.

Encouragement from the Psalms

This same God also desires that we look to him as our Father. What he manages to do for a nation that he calls his people, he longs to do for us as his children. He offers a closeness to us that is usually reserved for a family. He is more than a just judge or lawgiver; he offers personal protection for those who have drawn near to him for protection and blessing. These concepts of protection or safety combined with blessing have been appropriated by Christians from Old Testament texts throughout the history of the church. Many of the most memorable passages come from the Psalms.

The Psalms have always been a primary source of encouragement for Christians. Of those psalms that relate to God as Protector, Psalm 46 must rank near the top as one to turn to for precisely this kind of encouragement. This psalm may also be the most often sung, as Luther used it as the basis for his well-known hymn "A Might Fortress Is Our God." Here is Psalm 46 in its entirety, all eleven verses:

> [1] God is our refuge and strength,
> a very present help in trouble.
> [2] Therefore we will not fear though the earth gives way,
> though the mountains be moved into the heart of the sea,
> [3] though its waters roar and foam,
> though the mountains tremble at its swelling. *Selah*
>
> [4] There is a river whose streams make glad the city of God,
> the holy habitation of the Most High.
> [5] God is in the midst of her; she shall not be moved;
> God will help her when morning dawns.
> [6] The nations rage, the kingdoms totter;
> he utters his voice, the earth melts.
> [7] The Lord of hosts is with us;
> the God of Jacob is our fortress. *Selah*
>
> [8] Come, behold the works of the Lord,
> how he has brought desolations on the earth.
> [9] He makes wars cease to the end of the earth;
> he breaks the bow and shatters the spear;

he burns the chariots with fire.
[10] "Be still, and know that I am God.
I will be exalted among the nations,
I will be exalted in the earth!"
[11] The Lord of hosts is with us;
the God of Jacob is our fortress. *Selah*

The psalm simply oozes with confidence in God's protection and the courage which the resulting sense of safety brings. It begins with the positive statement, "God is our refuge and strength, a very present help in trouble." This is the essence of God as our Protector. He is a refuge, and much like the city of refuge in the book of Numbers, he is a safe place for us to run. He is our strength, implying that we are not the strong ones, he is. A very present help, the very thing we need when trouble comes upon us unexpectedly. And thanks to this assurance that God is the psalmist's refuge, he can make the courageous statement "we will not fear."

The psalmist's courage is not reserved for everyday mishaps. He is ready to display his valor in the face of almost any imaginable circumstance. Let the earth itself give way and let mountains be moved into the heart of the sea. The worst kind of natural disasters are no reason to let confidence in our Protector be diminished. He moves on to discuss the sea itself. The Israelites were not much of a seafaring people, so one could almost understand if the sea presented for some of them a particularly ominous potential source of calamity. But no, our author assures us. Let the sea's waters roar and foam, let it swell so that even the mountains tremble at its swelling. We will remain calm; we will keep looking to the Lord as our refuge.

The next stanza paints the picture of a city that is living in peace. The river of God runs through this city of God, making the inhabitants glad, while outside nations rage and kingdoms totter. The Lord brings stability to this community and protects these people from whatever troubles there might be among those who oppose them. Then the psalmist adds a refrain, "The Lord of hosts is with us; the God of Jacob is our fortress." We are safe not because we are strong, but because God is, and he is with us. He is our fortress. In a day of walled cities, a city and its fortress quality were intertwined. The ancient city simply *was* a kind of fortress.

Spiritual Warfare

At this point, I want to be sure to emphasize that the power is all God's and not ours. Whenever the Bible gets to those sections where God, through his inspired word, tells us what to do, we can easily fall into the trap of attempting to do things in our own strength, which never works. The right thing to do is to do the right thing, of course, while always reminding ourselves that we are completely relying upon him. All that we do as we serve God must fall into the category of Phil 2 12-13. "… work out your own salvation with fear and trembling, for it is God who works in you, both to will and to work for his good pleasure." We work while he works in us, to make us both willing and able to accomplish his will.

One major part of his will is that we effectively stand firm against the schemes of the devil. All the trials of this present world have a spiritual component. Were it not for the Fall of Adam and sin attaching itself to the very nature of our human race, we might surmise that there would be no trials or trouble at all. But that is at least partly conjecture. Reality is full of earthy trials and attacks with smaller or greater spiritual causes and implications. We are up against a spiritual adversary, and we need to fight him off. To do so, God offers us his armor.

The armor is his and he is the source of it, just as he is the source of everything that we need for the Christian life. So, as we do battle against the devil and his legions, God is doing battle in the heavenlies on our behalf. We can envision angels going head-to-head against demons, with God making sure the demons never finally get their way. All of this takes place in the supernatural realm while we go about our routines, read our Bibles, say our prayers, and get caught up in the challenges of an ordinary day. Yet, there is more to it than that.

God our Father no doubt protects us in more ways and more often than we will ever know. His providence is all-encompassing, and that means he has his eyes and hands on the details of our lives, orchestrating things that we might never understand even if we knew what he was doing. But he does not intend to do all his protecting of us while we are unconscious of it. He is always at work, but at the same time, he wants to work in ways that we can see, experience, and appreciate for ourselves, and this is where the armor of God comes in. Here is the text of Eph 6:10-18:

> Finally, be strong in the Lord and in the strength of his might. Put on the whole armor of God, that you may be able to stand against the schemes of the devil. For we do not wrestle against flesh and blood, but against the rulers, against the authorities, against the cosmic powers over this present darkness, against the spiritual forces of evil in the heavenly places. Therefore, take up the whole armor of God, that you may be able to withstand in the evil day, and having done all, to stand firm. Stand therefore, having fastened on the belt of truth, and having put on the breastplate of righteousness, and, as shoes for your feet, having put on the readiness given by the gospel of peace. In all circumstances take up the shield of faith, with which you can extinguish all the flaming darts of the evil one; and take the helmet of salvation, and the sword of the Spirit, which is the word of God, praying at all times in the Spirit, with all prayer and supplication. To that end, keep alert with all perseverance, making supplication for all the saints,

We need to take up that armor in specific ways, and as we do, we will fight off the devil, who is always looking for someone to gobble up. As Peter reminds us, "Be sober-minded; be watchful. Your adversary the devil prowls around like a roaring lion, seeking someone to devour. Resist him, firm in your faith, knowing that the same kinds of suffering are being experienced by your brotherhood throughout the world" (1 Pet 5:8-9). And James re-inforces, "Submit yourselves therefore to God. Resist the devil, and he will flee from you" (James 4:7). But now back to Paul and appropriating the armor of God.

As mentioned, God is the one who is strong, not us, which is why Paul is careful to say, "be strong in the Lord and in the strength of his might." Then he tells us how to do that. We must "Put on the whole armor of God, that you may be able to stand against the schemes of the devil." The devil is both incredibly smart and exceptionally cruel, and unlike Wile E. Coyote in the old Road Runner cartoons, his efforts do not always lead to him falling off a cliff and landing at the bottom of a canyon. He loses in the end, but on the way there, he takes far too many people with him along the path to destruction. And he is not working alone.

Paul goes on to tell us, "We do not wrestle against flesh and blood, but against the rulers, against the authorities, against the cosmic powers over this present darkness, against the spiritual forces of evil in the heavenly places." Have you ever felt as if the armies of hell were conspiring together to try to ruin your life? Or maybe your family or your church? Based on that last sentence from Paul, those feelings may not be a figment of your imagination.

If we need more evidence that the spiritual forces in heaven can impact humans here on earth, the words "rulers" and "author-ities" make an interesting word study. In this passage and others, the rulers and authorities are clearly spiritual entities. For another example, see Eph 3:10, "so that through the church the manifold wisdom of God might now be made known to the *rulers and au-thorities* in the heavenly places." At the same time, Paul uses the same words in writing to a younger pastor Timothy, now clearly with an earthly focus. "Remind them to be submissive to rulers and authorities, to be obedient, to be ready for every good work" (1 Tim 3:1). There are a few more examples we could look at, but the point is clear. The world we live in is a *spiritual* world; that is, it is connected to the spiritual realm, which we cannot see. That portion of the universe which we cannot see is every bit as real as that which we see, walk around in and touch. That is why we need the armor of God.

As Paul says, "Therefore take up the whole armor of God, that you may be able to withstand in the evil day, and having done all, to stand firm." Again, we need to "take up" this armor. It is something we do willingly and on purpose. There is an element of God's protection that does not just happen. In some sense, we *make it happen*. I do not expect to always know or be able to explain exactly how this tension works, between what we do and what God does. Still, when God says in his word to do something, then at some level, we are responsible. So, we'd better take up that armor of God. And Paul goes on to describe it.

Stand therefore, having fastened on the belt of truth, and having put on the breastplate of righteousness, and, as shoes for your feet, having put on the readiness given by the gospel of peace. The truth is a supernatural defense against the enemy's assortment of lies. We take up this belt by knowing and adhering to the truth. When it comes to righteousness, we must receive the righteousness of Christ, but more than that, we need to engage in righteous acts – in good works. The divine righteousness is credited to us at the moment of conversion. We, like Abraham, have righteousness accounted to us by faith. But there is more; a continuous walking in righteousness is part of the Christian life, not to build up merit before God, but to carry out his revealed will. *Doing righteousness* is part of the spiritual battle. Finally, let's not forget the gospel. Without the good news of Jesus Christ, we would all be lost. Keep it always on your mind and in your heart, as Paul was willing to say even late in his life, "The saying is trustworthy and deserving of full acceptance, that Christ Jesus came into the world to save sinners, of whom I am the foremost."

Paul continues, "In all circumstances take up the shield of faith, with which you can extinguish all the flaming darts of the evil one." In case you haven't noticed, the enemy will attack your faith. More often, he will attack *you* in ways that you never expected. When these "flaming darts" come flying at us, the shield of faith is there to give these fiery projectiles something to strike.

We let our faith absorb the blow or take the hit. When we cannot change dire circumstances, or hurtful events, having the faith to walk through the challenge and remain faithful is the protection that we need.

The next bit of armor is "the helmet of salvation." How do we take up the helmet of salvation? One way is by reminding ourselves that we are saved. There are certain people who seem to have an unhealthy fixation on the question of whether or not they are saved. I single out the "unhealthy" version of this question because there is also a way in which the query is good. Paul tells us, "Examine yourselves, to see whether you are in the faith. Test yourselves. Or do you not realize this about yourselves, that Jesus Christ is in you?—unless indeed you fail to meet the test!" (2 Cor 13:5). But I think the context demands that the examination yields some results. We are either in the faith or we are not.

If we are in the faith already, then the case is closed, and we need to get down to the business of living out that faith. Too many questions can keep us from putting on the helmet. Receive God's assurance that you are his child. Let the Holy Spirit cry out "Abba!" from deep within you. If we are perhaps not yet truly believers, then we must make it a point to yield our lives to Christ in faith.

Any person who is unsure of whether they have truly put their faith in Christ should consider the following. The Bible is quite clear that all of us have sinned and therefore stand in need of God's forgiveness. Romans 3:23 makes the simple statement, "for all have sinned and fall short of the glory of God." Later in the same book, the Apostle Paul explains, "but God shows his love for us in that while we were still sinners, Christ died for us." In other words, Christ's death was intended as a sacrifice for our sins. The price we owed as those who have sinned against a perfectly holy God has now been paid, simply because God loved us. He wanted to remove the obstacle of our sin which was the thing that prevented our relating closely to him. Another Apostle, John this time, points out that there must be a conscious receiving of Jesus, an intentional placing of our trust in him. "But to all who did receive him, who believed in his name, he gave the right to become children of God" (John 1:12). Anyone who has up until now been unsure of their status before God can begin a relationship with him by praying a simple prayer. This one will do:

> Dear heavenly Father, I know that I have sinned against you and need your forgiveness. And I believe that Jesus died for my sins when he died on that cross. I believe that he rose from the dead, conquering death for guilty mortals just like me. Please, heavenly Father, give me eternal life. Please fill me with your Holy Spirit and help me to live for you, to love you and to serve you. In Christ, Amen.

At this point, it would be helpful to digest another bit from Romans and the Apostle Paul. "[15]For you did not receive the spirit of slavery to fall back into fear, but you have received the Spirit of adoption as sons, by whom we cry, "Abba! Father!" [16]The Spirit himself bears witness with our spirit that we are children of God." Once we put our faith in Jesus, we need to get about the business of living for him. If we are willing, we never have to fear for our eternal souls. What we rather need to do is remind ourselves of the Holy Spirit's presence within us and receive the assurance that we are now God's children. We belong to God. And speaking of the Spirit, let us remember to take up his sword.

The last item in this full set of military equipment is "the sword of the Spirit, which is the word of God." I do not know of any way to take up this bit of armor other than through practices relating to the Scriptures. Therefore, I would ask you to please dig into the Bible as much as you can. Read it, listen to someone else reading it, repeat it to the point of memorization, and listen to it being taught by Bible teachers who actually believe it – not those who tend to undermine its authority. The better you know the Bible, the more the Holy Spirit will bring it to mind. He will do so in situations that you never expected. There is no substitute for the authentic, pure spiritual nourishment that comes through God's word.

Finally, "praying at all times in the Spirit, with all prayer and supplication. To that end, keep alert with all perseverance, making supplication for all the saints." I am certain that when I get to meet God face to face, I will be both flabbergasted by the ways he has answered my prayers that I never knew about, and simultaneously a bit remorseful that I did not pray more or better prayers. Prayer guided by God's word is certainly the best kind. We know his will through his word and this aids us in knowing how to pray. Once we are confident of what to pray for, then "praying at all times" is how we need to implement that high quality prayer. More than that, we need to employ "perseverance" because a prayer that we give up on before we know that God has answered it can wither into a wasted prayer. Prayer is one of the ways we get into the battle. It is one of the ways we receive God's protection. It is a way of taking the offensive rather than merely trying not to be a victim. Let's make the devil a victim for a change.

Now I do not say that lightly. Our enemy is strong, and we need to be aware of his tactics. We need to rely on God's strength and trust in his character as our Father. Moreover, we cannot always expect to be at the top of our game. My lizard brain sends my emotions into wacky places too often, so I have to continually remind myself that I am, in fact, safe. Thankfully, we have a God who will protect us. We should praise him for it. Psalm 68:4-5 says:

> Sing to God, sing praises to his name;
> lift up a song to him who rides through the deserts;
> his name is the Lord;
> exult before him!
> Father of the fatherless and protector of widows
> is God in his holy habitation.

Let's also be committed to the practice of not giving into fear but remembering that God our Father is our Protector. He shall win the battle against Satan, while his intentions for us are only good. The enemy's days will come to an end and his ending is not going to be a happy one. Martin Luther in his hymn shows us what to hope for in this area. Let's close this chapter with more of his words:

> And though this world, with devils filled,
> Should threaten to undo us,
> We will not fear, for God hath willed
> His truth to triumph through us.
> The Prince of Darkness grim,—
> We tremble not for him;
> His rage we can endure,
> For lo! His doom is sure,—
> One little word shall fell him.

Amen, and all praise be to our Protector, our God and Father. He will always be there for us, which is more than we can say of our earthly fathers, or our mothers. We will now look at the (mostly hypothetical) chance that a mother will forget her son.

CHAPTER 10
THE FORGETFUL MOTHER

"We want desperately to believe that every mother falls in love with her baby at first sight and that the complexity of relationships, so evident elsewhere as part of the human condition, is totally absent from the connection between mother and child."
– Peg Streep, *Mean Mothers: Overcoming the Legacy of Hurt*

This chapter may not precisely relate to God's Fatherhood as the others do, but it does connect to the topic from my personal perspective. It is part of that larger voyage toward a better understanding of the Fatherhood of God and for plumbing the depth of that biblical truth we can all so easily miss.

There is a passage of Scripture, which I have thought about repeatedly, and it is found in Isaiah 49. Although I had certainly read it numerous times, there came a day when I *stumbled* and had to take a closer look. I must have been thinking at that moment of my own childhood history, when, during some routine daily Bible reading, this section stood out like it never had before. It deals with the restoration of Zion, which explains why I could have read it over and over without seeing any personal connection. The application of these verses can go well beyond the immediate context, since the passage clearly reveals God's character in a way that is uniquely encouraging.

An Excerpt from Isaiah 49

    Here is the passage in its entirety, beginning with a command to rejoice and ending with a reassuring promise:

> [13] Sing for joy, O heavens, and exult, O earth;
> break forth, O mountains, into singing!
> For the Lord has comforted his people
> and will have compassion on his afflicted.
> [14] But Zion said, "The Lord has forsaken me;
> my Lord has forgotten me."
> [15] "Can a woman forget her nursing child,
> that she should have no compassion on the son of her womb?
> Even these may forget,
> yet I will not forget you.
> [16] Behold, I have engraved you on the palms of my hands;
> your walls are continually before me.
> [17] Your builders make haste;
> your destroyers and those who laid you waste go out from you.
> [18] Lift up your eyes around and see;
> they all gather, they come to you.
> As I live, declares the Lord,
> you shall put them all on as an ornament;
> you shall bind them on as a bride does.
> [19] "Surely your waste and your desolate places
> and your devastated land—
> surely now you will be too narrow for your inhabitants,
> and those who swallowed you up will be far away.
> [20] The children of your bereavement
> will yet say in your ears:
> 'The place is too narrow for me;
> make room for me to dwell in.'
> [21] Then you will say in your heart:

'Who has borne me these?
I was bereaved and barren,
exiled and put away,
but who has brought up these?
Behold, I was left alone;
from where have these come?'"
²² Thus says the Lord God:
"Behold, I will lift up my hand to the nations,
and raise my signal to the peoples;
and they shall bring your sons in their arms,
and your daughters shall be carried on their shoulders.
²³ Kings shall be your foster fathers,
and their queens your nursing mothers.
With their faces to the ground they shall bow down to
you,
and lick the dust of your feet.
Then you will know that I am the Lord;
those who wait for me shall not be put to shame." (Isa
49:13-23)

Mother and Child – and God

God is in the business of bringing joy and rejoicing out of sit-uations that are outwardly or inwardly sad as can be. In this case, we read, "But Zion said, 'The Lord has forsaken me; my Lord has forgotten me.'" Jerusalem has seen some rough times over the years, and this was one of those times. During chronic trials and troubles, when our hope level is at low tide, it is easy to think that God is completely occupied with someone else. It's like calling customer service and being placed on an interminable hold. "Are you there, God? And if so, do you care, or are you just hoping I will hang up and go away?"

We know, however, that God has no intention of leaving Je-rusalem in its misery forever. As long and as hard as it seems, this is just a temporary delay. God wants his people to know that and encourages them to begin rejoicing even now. In fact, he wants heaven and earth and the mountains to all join in. The odds of God *not* intervening on his people's behalf are not even worth considering. He will do so, and this is more certain than just about anything we can imagine.

God asks Zion the hypothetical question, "Can a woman forget her nursing child, that she should have no compassion on the son of her womb?" The expected answer to this question is, "Of course not! How silly to even think of such a thing." What mother could ignore her child, and her infant child at that? It is uncommon, but sometimes something much like this happens. I must confess I have wondered whether something like this applied to me. Before I even knew that I was the third child of my mother given away at birth and ultimately adopted, I wondered. More precisely, I wondered if my original mother thought about me. Probably so, though how often and with what kind of thoughts I cannot say. Sometimes I wondered if she gave me a name, known only to herself, one which never made it onto the original birth certificate. I also wondered if she ever saw me after giving birth that day in Deaconess Hospital in Buffalo before I went home with another family. I have never known if I was with my adoptive parents in court on the day that I became legally theirs, and if so, whether Frances Kosciolek was there too along with Casimir and Florence Kosobucki, to sign off on documents or to hear the approval of the judge.

Unlikely as it is for a woman to forget her child, it does happen, in a way. Women may at least try to forget, for most practical purposes, the children to which they have given birth. In some cases, it may be the only way to cope with reality. Perhaps my own natural mother tried to forget me and my siblings as a way of coping, since she no longer had legal access to us. In speaking with both my birth mother's former coworker and next-door neighbor, neither said they knew that Frances had any children. Her own sister knew only of me, but not the first two babies. The times were such that no one would have ever acknowledged that seeing us or knowing us could truly be helpful for her or her children. God is different.

God admits it can happen in extreme cases but asserts firmly that it will never happen to Zion. By extension, I believe it is safe to say it will never happen to any child of his. He states this with the words, "Even these may forget, yet I will not forget you. Behold, I have engraved you on the palms of my hands." God is clear that he loves Zion more than a mother loves her infant child. Knowing God's heart for widows and orphans, we can be confident that he loves the fatherless – and motherless – child in much the same way. The picture of being engraved on the hands of God speaks partly of permanence, but also of a method of drawing attention to something that cannot be ignored.

There are more and less permanent ways of remembering, such as tying a string around a finger, or writing notes in ink on the back of a hand. More permanent would be a tattoo. When people do get a tattoo of their sweetheart's name, it may intentionally go somewhere where others can see it, or somewhere discreet so few people see it at all. But how about engraving – tattooing – a person's name on the palms (plural) of your hands? You would be forced to look at it all the time. God could not forget Israel and cannot forget us if he tried.

What a reassuring thought this is! The orphan child, who fears she may be forgotten by her mother, who feels sure he is forgotten by his father, is constantly, persistently nagging on the mind of God. God would have it no other way. He loves the orphan. He loves the fatherless or motherless child. He loves you, me, and us with a love that urges him chronically to take care of our every need. For those of us whose lives have been characterized by instability or uncertainty in the realm of family relationships, there is no more uplifting idea than to be perpetually on the mind of a loving, heavenly Father. He does not care for us in some abstract way, like those who love humanity but seem to dislike the actual people that they meet. He is highly motivated to address each concern that crosses our every path.

In the case of Jerusalem, it was the walls. On each of the many occasions when the city has been destroyed, God looked on in deeply involved pity and made the city whole again.

Someday the rebuilding will be permanent and take the form of the New Jerusalem we find in the Bible's last book. For the orphan child, who may now be all grown up, but whose life is in ruins, God will gaze down in compassion and rebuild that broken life, restore that broken heart. If trusting God has been difficult, are we willing to trust him again? This has been a repeated theme in these reflections and there is good reason for it. It is one component of the gospel that the fatherless child, whose heart may now be calloused against trust as a protective measure, needs to take to heart again and again. Eventually, it will become a habit, a more natural disposition, to trust in our heavenly Father.

God promises in the Isaiah passage to eventually send the destroyers of Jerusalem packing. He also looks to the future and promises children to Zion that the city is poorly equipped to recognize. All of this speaks to a future full of love, hope, security and belonging. Dare we set our sights on this kind of future? It may be hard to believe, but God wants us to believe it. It is one way of expressing our trust in him.

No More Shame

After more promises of honor, the passage ends with "Then you will know that I am the Lord; those who wait for me shall not be put to shame." Does this not describe what we are longing for deep in the center of our souls? We want the confidence to rest in the reality that the God we know is the God who really cares for us and not some imposter who is going to pull the rug out from under us in the end. We also want the assurance that our lives, our futures, and our eternities will not end in the depths of some new cause for shame. Shame is a beguiling problem. In the words of Ed Welch, a well-known Christian counselor:

> Shame is the deep sense that you are unacceptable because of something you did, something done to you or something associated with you.

Or, to strengthen the language,
You are disgraced because you acted less than human, you
were treated as if you were less than human, or you were
associated with something less than human, and there are
witnesses. [17]

Curt Thompson, an MD who blends the science of neurobiol-
ogy with spirituality, offers an additional, perhaps more technical
perspective, saying we can understand shame as "an undercurrent
of sensed emotion, of which we may have either a slight or robust
impression that, should we put words to it, would declare some
version of *I am not enough; There is something wrong with me; I
am bad;* or *I don't matter.*" [18]

All of this is what God promises not to let overtake us if we
only will wait for him. If you are like me, you have regularly felt
like this. Maybe it has described a great part of your existence. I
was ashamed that I was adopted, because, well, I was never sure
why. I mainly knew that it was something to be ashamed of, something not to be spoken of in public. I was ashamed that my adopted
mother could not read and write, as it reflected upon both of us
badly. Part of that particular shame was due to my unsuccessful
attempts to teach her. Looking back, I was a teenager at the time,
making the expectations unrealistic, even with the help of a litera-
cy volunteer, who was never to be mentioned to anyone. Still, the
tentacles of this multi-layered shame reached in from many different directions. They were long and grasped at me constantly and
they stung. Shame was, for all practical purposes, inescapable. Or
so I thought. It turns out I was wrong.

God's Final Word

If we wait for God to rescue us, we shall not be put to shame.
Shame cannot have the last word. The universe is constructed,

---

17 Edward T. Welch, *Shame Interrupted: How God Lifts the Pain of Worthlessness
and Rejection* (Greensboro, New Growth Press, 2012), 2.
18 Curt Thompson, M., *The Soul of Shame: Retelling the Stories We Believe about
Ourselves.* (Downers Grove: IVP Books, 2015), 24.

and Christ's sacrifice is precisely targeted, in such a way that God gains the final victory over all the shame that might ever fall upon us or might well up from within. He will certainly never let himself be put to shame when the final curtain falls. That is why Jesus died when and where and in the way that he did. The shame that Christ endured on the cross eliminates every bit of the shame that torments us, whether we were the source of it ourselves or it was somehow inflicted by others. Curt Thompson reminds us that "shame does not get the final word in the story that Jesus is telling – the one he invites us to participate in as coauthors, the one in which God's delight commands our attention far more than does our shame." [19] We need to focus on Jesus' version of the story, rather than on the one that we may have been telling ourselves for so long.

Ed Welch gives us some instructions as to how to use God's version of the story to work on renewing our minds. He says:

> Identify shame, hear God's words and believe them, take a journey past death into eternity itself until your soul is full and you are confident that joy has the last word. Then come back to the challenges of today. It sounds like one big loop, but once you get back to everyday life, everything looks different after you've had a glimpse of heaven. You know who wins. [20]

The child who has tried to navigate life in a big, mean world alone, without adequate help from parents, cannot be expected to succeed. If you believe your father has abandoned you and mother has forgotten you, it may feel as if there is no way the story can end well. You may have tried to make it work as best as you could, with that chip on your shoulder and a searing pain in your heart, but still failed. So now you are additionally ashamed of that failure. Further, you are ashamed because the story as you have told it to yourself cannot be rewritten. The good news is that we do not

19 Thompson, *The Soul of Shame,* 187
20 Welch, *Shame Interrupted,* 324

even need that old story. We have access to a different, bigger and better story.

When God incorporates our story into his, it all turns out well. He and his story are both big enough to include us and our stories, twisted as they are, and bring them around to a happy ending with all the loose ends tied up. He has comforted his people and had compassion on his afflicted. We shall not be forsaken or forgotten in the end. We matter to him even if we never mattered enough to anyone else in the past. He is the best Father of all – so good in fact that he more than makes up for the father or mother we never had. This is a remarkable truth that we need to let sink in.

God will not forget us. He will not abandon us. It is not in his nature and is, therefore, something he cannot do. If our lives seem to have fallen apart and we know that at least some of that mess is due to circumstances beyond our control, we can look to our heavenly Father and know that nothing is beyond his control. The one who placed the stars in the heavens and cares for the birds is looking out for us. We, like Zion, are engraved on the palms of his hands. Whatever walls need to be rebuilt, he will see to it that the workers are available and fully equipped to get the job done. Our eternity is safe, and not because we can do enough to make it so. Nor do we need to rely upon people much like those who have been unfaithful in the past. Our trust is in a faithful Creator who looks upon us with the heart of a caring Father.

While there may be mothers who forget their children, rare as it may be, there is nothing that escapes God's notice. There is nothing that falls beyond the scope of his eternal plan. His existence was eternal before time began, he already sees into eternity future and has given us just enough of a glimpse to know he is there. If we keep our eyes fixed upon him and the eternal glory that he has prepared for us, we can face whatever we need to face here and now. That which we face today is small and temporary compared with all that God our Father has under his control. Having contrasted God with a negligent mother, we will now look at Jesus as the obedient Son.

CHAPTER 11
THE OBEDIENT SON

*"As Adam's disobedience made us sinners,
the obedience of Christ makes us righteous.
We owe everything to the obedience of Christ."*
– Andrew Murray, *The School of Obedience*

Obedience is going completely out of fashion. Rebellion, which has long been attractive for many, is now more stylish than ever before. For reasons that are probably too complex to dig into here, the whole idea of submitting to someone in authority precisely because they have authority has changed its tone. It can no longer be considered an expression of loyalty or of understanding the chain of command. Any exercise of authority seems like an abuse of that authority. Obedience to authority is then giving in to that abuse. Authority now rests in the hands of the mob, not with the traditional authority figure.

If we take that perspective and apply it to our understanding of God, we find ourselves with a God who is abusive, out to demean us and tear us apart. On the other hand, we may reject that God and decide on a tame *god* who answers to us and does what we ask. We get either something close to a devil who wants to destroy us or a fairy godmother who grants our wishes. Neither of these is God as he has revealed himself in Scripture.

In the Bible, God is authoritative and expects to be obeyed. Andrew Murray laid it out nicely in his *School of Obedience*.

"The Father in heaven asks, requires, and expects all of His children to give Him wholehearted and entire obedience all day long, every single day." [21] Murray is right, but that is a tall order and none of us can live up to it without God's help. Yet, with or without God's help, this is precisely the kind of God we tend, these days, to reject. That rejection is mainly misguided.

The Original Rebellion

If we reject the God of the Bible without really understanding him, we have rejected the true God based on a falsehood. If we see God as an abusive authority figure, then we are in a sense, believing the original lie. In Gen 3:1-5, we find the story:

> Now the serpent was more cunning than any beast of the field which the Lord God had made. And he said to the woman, "Has God indeed said, 'You shall not eat of every tree of the garden'?"
>
> And the woman said to the serpent, "We may eat the fruit of the trees of the garden; but of the fruit of the tree which is in the midst of the garden, God has said, 'You shall not eat it, nor shall you touch it, lest you die.'"
>
> Then the serpent said to the woman, "You will not surely die. For God knows that in the day you eat of it your eyes will be opened, and you will be like God, knowing good and evil."

In other words, the *abusive authority* falsehood is precisely the lie that the serpent wanted Eve to believe, and alas, she fell for it, Adam followed her, and we all pay the price. What if God was not abusive? What if he was not trying to keep us from that which is good? What if we really had a different kind of God altogether?

---

21 Andrew Murray, Andrew, *The School of Obedience*. Kindle Edition. (Abbottsford: Aneko Press, 2019) Kindle, in the Preface.

The Logic of Obedience

The God that we find in the Bible is all-knowing and all-powerful. In him, that knowledge and power are combined with love for us beyond measure, and a limitless longing to see only that which works toward our benefit. This God knows you and me at a level so intimate that only the One who created us can know us so well. It is a knowledge and understanding that digs down to subatomic detail while also comprehending our biggest hopes and wildest dreams. And this knowledge is what makes authority not abusive, but caring while being altogether acquainted with us.

Obedience, when given to the God who really exists, is then a warm and loving act given in return for his loving attention. One reason religious people may be attracted to law as opposed to grace is that law makes obedience less personal. We can keep up certain religious practices and allow them to turn into mindless habits. We might pray at certain times using specific words, and all the while hold God at a distance. Others may see us as very devout and when we look in the mirror, there may be days when we are satisfied with what we see. Then we might compare ourselves to others and keep score. All of this will have nothing whatsoever in common with the intimate relationship with God we described above – and nothing in common with obedience. How very different this is from Jesus!

A Look at the Obedience of Christ

Christ's obedience was all encompassing. It was also one of a kind, detailed, and personal. He outwardly kept the law more thoroughly than anyone before or since, although admittedly his maintaining of the human tradition connected with that law fell short at times – and intentionally so, it seems. He loved to irritate those bound by tradition. Still, at the core of his obedient behavior was the intimate relationship he had with his Father, and this relationship was unique to him. God the Son, while walking this earth in human flesh, stayed close to God his Father in heaven.

John states it like this in his prologue, "No one has ever seen God; the only God [or *Son*], who is at the Father's side, he has made him known (John 1:18). Or again, later in John, "not that anyone has seen the Father except he who is from God; he has seen the Father" (John 6:46). Christ knew his Father better than anyone else could ever know him and his obedience was complete. "And he who sent me is with me. He has not left me alone, for I always do the things that are pleasing to him" (John 8:29). Always. In Psalm 40:6-8 we get a prophetic description:

> In sacrifice and offering you have not delighted,
> but you have given me an open ear.
> Burnt offering and sin offering
> you have not required.
> Then I said, "Behold, I have come;
> in the scroll of the book it is written of me:
> I delight to do your will, O my God;
> your law is within my heart."

David contrasts the giving of sacrifice to a life of obedience. This is in the spirit of what the Prophet Samuel says in response to Saul, who evidently felt sacrifice was the main thing. "And Samuel said, 'Has the Lord as great delight in burnt offerings and sacrifices, as in obeying the voice of the Lord? Behold, to obey is better than sacrifice, and to listen than the fat of rams.'"

The "open ear" given by God in the psalm is, in Hebrew, something more like "ears you have dug for me." The word "open" or "dug" is related to Psalm 22:16, "they have *pierced* my hands and feet," as the soldier did, piercing the Savior's hand and feet with nails. When we transfer that thought back to the ears of Psalm 40, we are reminded of the piercing of the ear of the bondservant in Deuteronomy 15:12-17:

> If your brother, a Hebrew man or a Hebrew woman, is sold to you, he shall serve you six years, and in the seventh year you shall let him go free from you. And when

you let him go free from you, you shall not let him go empty-handed. You shall furnish him liberally out of your flock, out of your threshing floor, and out of your wine-press. As the Lord your God has blessed you, you shall give to him. You shall remember that you were a slave in the land of Egypt, and the Lord your God redeemed you; therefore I command you this today. But if he says to you, 'I will not go out from you,' because he loves you and your household, since he is well-off with you, then you shall take an awl, and put it through his ear into the door, and he shall be your slave forever. And to your female slave you shall do the same.

This is no naïve or halfhearted obedience. When a slave willingly had his ear pierced out of love and loyalty to his master, he meant business. It was a lifelong commitment to doing the master's will. This sheds light on the prophetically spoken words of the coming Messiah a bit later in the psalm, "I delight to do your will, O my God; your law is within my heart." There is no desire here to substitute sacrifice for obedience, to let an animal die while the rebel puts on a religious show. This is obedience through and through, given willingly and given with joy. This is the kind of obedience the Son gave to the Father. And in Hebrews it is brought up again. This time the wording is a bit different, as it is taken from the LXX, the Greek translation of the Hebrew Bible, the version that was most accessible to the early church. Here it is from Hebrews 10:4-7, with a little context to set up the quotation from the Psalms:

> For it is impossible for the blood of bulls and goats to take away sins. Consequently, when Christ came into the world, he said,
> "Sacrifices and offerings you have not desired,
> but a body have you prepared for me;
> in burnt offerings and sin offerings
> you have taken no pleasure.

Then I said, 'Behold, I have come to do your will, O God, as it is written of me in the scroll of the book.'"

Two things stand out from this passage when we relate it back to the Old Testament passages that we have looked at already. The first is, "it is impossible for the blood of bulls and goats to take away sins." In other words, the sacrifices never cleansed the hearts and souls of those who offered them. Bulls and goats are an inadequate substitute for a human who has sinned against God. They only pointed to a better sacrifice that would one day eventually come. It came in the Person of Jesus.

If we look back at the quotation in Hebrews, taken from the LXX, we see a little change. The opened or pierced ears that reminded us of the bondservant in Deuteronomy have been replaced by the words, "a body have you prepared for me." The obedience of Christ was not expressed with a pierced ear, but with the pierced hands and feet of crucifixion. At the Last Supper he was able to say, "This is my body, which is given for you" (Luke 22:19). His whole body went to the cross. His obedience was total. "I have come to do your will, O God." That was how Christ's ministry looked at the end of the Gospels, and we will consider this even more a bit later, but there was obedience the whole way through.

Christ's Obedient Life

If we want to know what complete obedience looks like, we can look at the complete life of Jesus. His life was full of compassion and patience, but he was never complacent with sin. He seemingly made time for every interruption, but there were also times when he left or ignored the crowds to spend time alone. For Jesus, *alone* meant time with his Father. And it was the Father to whom Jesus was always obedient. Always. I am not sure what exactly this sort of constant obedience would look like in my own life, but at least we have Christ's life to look at to give us a starting point.

Let's begin with his childhood. In Luke 2:46-51, we find a story that comes from Christ's youth. He had gone with his family to Jerusalem and now they were on their way back, well, at least his family was:

> After three days they found him in the temple, sitting among the teachers, listening to them and asking them questions. And all who heard him were amazed at his understanding and his answers. And when his parents saw him, they were astonished. And his mother said to him, "Son, why have you treated us so? Behold, your father and I have been searching for you in great distress." And he said to them, "Why were you looking for me? Did you not know that I must be in my Father's house?" And they did not understand the saying that he spoke to them. And he went down with them and came to Nazareth and was submissive to them. And his mother treasured up all these things in her heart.

In the above story Christ displays two forms of obedience – or obedience to two different authorities. The first is to his Father in heaven, the second to his parents on earth. These two were not meant to be in conflict, like two rival bosses vying for an employee's time. Obedience to the one was obedience to the other, with God the Father being the authority over both parents and the divine Child.

When Jesus says that he must be "in my Father's house" or "about my Father's business" as it also worded, he is indicating an understood compliance to the will of God the Father. His place was in the temple with the teachers, even though he was only about twelve years of age at the time. In his mind, this was as perfectly natural a thing as could be imagined. Where else would he rather be? His Father's house was his home. Discussions on the law and the prophets or theological Q&A would have been a comfort zone for this astute adolescent. We can only imagine what those conversations were like, but there is another form of obedience about which Luke informs us.

In the final verse of the passage, Luke tells us that Jesus "went down with them [his parents] and came to Nazareth and was submissive to them." This may be more remarkable than the previous example. It is one thing to be submissive to a perfectly holy, perfectly loving, all-knowing and all-powerful God. To be submissive to even the best of this world's normal, everyday, flawed individuals is another thing entirely. This is, of course, what children are called to do. Paul writes in Gal 6:1-3, "Children, obey your parents in the Lord, for this is right. 'Honor your father and mother' (this is the first commandment with a promise), 'that it may go well with you and that you may live long in the land.'" Still, in the case of the rest of us humans, we are just as flawed as our parents and our children are just as flawed as we are. Jesus was God before the incarnation and remained so even at this early age. I am not quite sure how Christ gave that kind of honor to Mary and Joseph, but since it was Jesus, it must have been a beautiful thing to behold. Who of us can say that as a teenager we were submissive to our parents?

In my case, it was at about this age that I lost my adoptive father. Prior to that, I do not think "submissive" would have been the perfect word to describe my relationship with him. I mainly remember just trying to stay out of his way. As for my mother, I probably do not have the right word in my sizable vocabulary to describe that relationship, but again, "submissive" would never work. Yet in Christ's case, it is the only word Luke uses to frame the attitude and behavior that Jesus displayed in the home of Mary and Joseph through his youthful years. Even in those moments when his deity was seeping out through his humanity, and the fact that he was their Creator as well as their son was somehow evident, he still managed to be the obedient son that any parent might be pleased with. They could be proud of him and enjoy their happy home.

As he got older and set out to accomplish his ministry, Jesus was still obedient to the Father in heaven. This is evident in the fact that he seemed always to know just what to do and when to do it. Of course, this tendency was consistently supported by prayer. Take this passage from the Gospel of Luke, "And when it was day, he departed and went into a desolate place. And the people sought him and came to him, and would have kept him from leaving them, but he said to them, 'I must preach the good news of the kingdom of God to the other towns as well; for I was sent for this purpose.' And he was preaching in the synagogues of Judea" (Luke 4:42-44). What is interesting here is that Jesus prioritizes certain people over others. There are those who "sought him and came to him and would have kept him from leaving them" and then there are the people in the "other towns." Jesus needed to move on for he was "sent for this purpose." He was sent by his Father with particular goals or objectives in mind.

The whole fact that Jesus was "sent" put him in an obedient role. Comparing himself to John the Baptist, who was also sent by God, Jesus said, "But the testimony that I have is greater than that of John. For the works that the Father has given me to accomplish, the very works that I am doing, bear witness about me that the Father has sent me" (John 5:36). The works Jesus did were from the Father, and they bore witness to the fact that Christ was sent. Every part of this speaks of obedience on the part of Christ. He was sent, so he came to earth out of obedience. He came to accomplish particular works which the Father gave him to do. God the Son is obedient to God the Father.

The Father and the Son

Keep in mind that Jesus Christ, God the Son, is still God. Over us he has absolute authority. But though the Father, Son and Spirit interacted prior to Christ's coming to earth, it is not easy for us to imagine precisely how they related to one another in their eternal Trinitarian state. Once on earth, however, we know this much from Heb 5:8-9, "Although he was a son, he learned obedience through what he suffered. And being made perfect, he became the source of eternal salvation to all who obey him." It is difficult to say, but perhaps a loving, submissive relationship had little reason to obey when the divine Persons were all that there was. As he entered the created order, Christ "learned obedience" from the human perspective. This gives us an example embedded in the source of our salvation. Now as we submit to Christ, we also submit to our heavenly Father. There is something in taking on the right attitude, an attitude of submission and obedience, that allows us to grow closer to Christ and the Father. I am thinking of an interaction Jesus had in the Gospel of John.

Our Will and God's Will

As Jesus began teaching in Jerusalem at the temple, some of the Jews began to ask questions. Here it is from John 7:14-17, "About the middle of the feast Jesus went up into the temple and began teaching. The Jews therefore marveled, saying, "How is it that this man has learning, when he has never studied?" So Jesus answered them, "My teaching is not mine, but his who sent me. If anyone's will is to do God's will, he will know whether the teaching is from God or whether I am speaking on my own authority."

There is more than one thing here to consider. First, Christ's teaching is from the Father. Occasionally one hears poorly informed people, even Christians, contrast the Father and the Son as if they differed in their teaching or in their will. Nothing could be further from the truth. The very things Jesus taught came from the Father himself. For us to know this, we have to take on the attitude that Jesus also had, and that is an attitude of submission, which is our next point.

Jesus describes it as "If anyone's will is to do God's will." That is how the ESV puts it. The NET says, "If anyone wants to do God's will." Finally, the NIV words it, "Anyone who chooses to do the will of God." All of this speaks of a willing attitude on our part to begin with, which may or may not have been present in the individual Jews who were questioning Jesus that day. But if we start with that willing heart, then we, according to Jesus, "will know whether the teaching is from God or whether I am speaking on my own authority." This tells me that we come to know both Jesus and the Father better through our own attitude of obedience.

I wonder if a lot of our sense of feeling distant from God might go away if we simply decided to submit our will to his. We cannot artificially work up the warm fuzzy feelings we may hope for that are connected to knowing God as a Father, especially if we are unsure what having a Father feels like to start off. We might long for that sense of belonging entailed in being God's daughter or God's son – and we might imagine that feeling we belong would lead to more perfect obedience on our part. It might, but we cannot wait for feelings of belonging to engulf us before we decide to obey.

To know the heart of God the Father as expressed in the teaching of Christ, we should start with an attitude of obedience. We need a desire to do God's will, and lest we think that this desire must be some unachievable, holy longing that seems to elude us, we can take it from the NIV's wording of John 7:17, "Anyone who chooses to do the will of God will find out whether my teaching comes from God or whether I speak on my own." We may not be full of holy longings, but we can certainly choose to do the will of God, while the desires still may, well, leave something to be desired. At some later point, we may seriously hope that the whole concept of obedience to the will of God might begin to make a lot more sense. Obedience might come more naturally because we know God better and we might get to know him better through our attitude of obedience. So where do we start?

The Fruit of the Spirit v. the Works of the Flesh (and the Law)

I propose we start by spotlighting the fruit of the Spirit, which Paul contrasts with the works of the flesh in Galatians. The qualities mentioned, such as love, joy, peace, etc., all seem like attitudes or dispositions. Focusing on such things that originate with the Spirit within us will help us avoid practices that can fall into simple legalism, such as "Read/pray so much per day," or "Do these five things." What I find both fascinating and helpful is that Paul contrasts the fruit not only with the works of the flesh but with the law. That contrast with the law means that there is an outward element. Let's read the following closely to see what Paul means:

> But I say, walk by the Spirit, and you will not gratify the desires of the flesh. For the desires of the flesh are against the Spirit, and the desires of the Spirit are against the flesh, for these are opposed to each other, to keep you from doing the things you want to do. But if you are led by the Spirit, you are not under the law. Now the works of the flesh are evident: sexual immorality, impurity, sensuality, idolatry, sorcery, enmity, strife, jealousy, fits of anger, rivalries, dissensions, divisions, envy, drunkenness, orgies, and things like these. I warn you, as I warned you before, that those who do such things will not inherit the kingdom of God.

> But the fruit of the Spirit is love, joy, peace, patience, kindness, goodness, faithfulness, gentleness, self-control; against such things there is no law. And those who belong to Christ Jesus have crucified the flesh with its passions and desires. If we live by the Spirit, let us also keep in step with the Spirit. (Gal 5:16-29)

Again, the fruit of the Spirit is contrasted with the works of the flesh, but then both before and after his lists of vices and virtues Paul says, "But if you are led by the Spirit, you are not under the law," and then again, "against such things there is no law." Paul wants us to know we are on safe ground when we cultivate the fruit of the Spirit whether inwardly, in our hearts, or outwardly in our active lives. Each type of fruit is part of walking in the Spirit.

That is precisely where Paul begins, "But I say, walk by the Spirit, and you will not gratify the desires of the flesh." If we are trying to dampen the desires of the flesh so that they no longer have a hold on us, we can do so by walking by the Spirit. Paul gives us two easy reference lists so that we can turn here to get an idea of *what* and *what not* to do. We need not focus too much here on the works of the flesh, which indeed are evident. We know what they are, perhaps by experience. Do take notice, however, of Paul's word of caution, "I warn you, as I warned you before, that those who do such things will not inherit the kingdom of God." That is worded strongly enough to let us know that these things are not part of the Christian life. Their presence means we are not walking by the Spirit, so it is helpful to identify them.

Here is that list once again. Let's read through it a make a mental note which of these have given us trouble: "sexual immorality, impurity, sensuality, idolatry, sorcery, enmity, strife, jealousy, fits of anger, rivalries, dissensions, divisions, envy, drunkenness, orgies, and things like these." We probably do not struggle in all these areas, but we likely struggle in more than one. A regular prayer for God's help to avoid these besetting issues can do wonders. By regular, I mean several times a day. As Paul says, "These are opposed to each other, to keep you from doing the things you want to do." Any giving in to the desires of the flesh will hinder the Spirit's production of fruit from within us. Therefore, we should focus on the positive qualities of Spirit-empowered, life-giving fruit.

Before we discuss how the fruit is produced, there is one error we need to avoid. I have repeatedly heard, and no doubt said a few times, that you never see a tree struggling to produce its fruit. Provide it with the right conditions, we say, and the fruit will most certainly come. This is true at a certain level, but we dare not compare humans with trees in every way. Trees, we may safely assume, never deliberately disobey God. They suffer from disease, malnutrition, or dehydration, but they do not rise up and rebel. We humans are different.

We have been rebelling since the Garden of Eden, so when we think in terms of the tree analogy, we need to set ourselves some limits. Yes, give us the right conditions and the fruit will come. Stay in the Scriptures, in prayer, and in fellowship with other believers in a Bible-teaching local church. Look for available ministry opportunities and step out in faith. As we do these things, fruit will appear, but normally this happens as long as we willingly take concrete steps. That is part of what I believe it means to "walk by the Spirit" or "keep in step with the Spirit."

The Spirit desires to form in us the qualities of "love, joy, peace, patience, kindness, goodness, faithfulness, gentleness, self-control." If we want to keep in step with him, then we must also desire to see these qualities formed. One way we can work at this is to pick one *piece of fruit* each morning and keep repeating it as we go through our day. "The fruit of the Spirit is love," we might say, or "The fruit of the Spirit is faithfulness." Then on that given day, we look for opportunities to express love, or faithfulness, or self-control, or whatever. I have found that when I do this, the Spirit provides me an opportunity to make good on my commitment. I can express love in word and/or deed. A chance will come up in which I can purposefully be faithful, gentle, or kind. This, we may now observe, is walking in obedience to God.

Jesus was obedient to his Father and we ought to express obedience to him too. If we have never quite understood how to be obedient to an earthly father, or were denied the opportunity to learn, there is still hope. Cultivating the fruit of the Spirit is not the only way to express our obedience, but it is a start. And it is something that we can all do. It is also personal and character-based, which helps us avoid the trap of legalism even as we try to squash and then eliminate those ugly works of the flesh.

Obedience Like That of Jesus

We have seen that Christ's obedience was total. God expects our obedience to be the same. We may fall short. Okay, we *will* fall short, but we are not allowed to look for excuses. When we fall short, we seek forgiveness instead. Yet, it is not asking too much to incline our hearts toward the Father with a deep desire and intention to grow in our obedience to him. We do not need warm fuzzy feelings to start out, which is nice because we may not get them. We need a willingness to do the Father's will. Then we will understand the teachings of Christ and the character of our loving

God and Father. Having seen Christ's obedience throughout his life, we will now look at his obedience to the end – to the very moment he was forsaken by the Father while on the cross.

CHAPTER 12
FORSAKEN BY HIS FATHER

"The Son of God suffered unto the death, not that men might not suffer, but that their sufferings might be like His."
– George Macdonald, *Unspoken Sermons,* First Series, used by C. S. Lewis as the epigraph for his book, *The Problem of Pain*

The fatherless child gets few advantages in this world. One of them is found in the perspective gained while considering the death of Christ. The orphan knows what it means to be forsaken, to have no one respond in a time of need. Christ knows this yearning heartache at least as well as we do, and he knows it from the agony of experience. In Matt 27:46, while he is hanging on the cross, we read, "And about the ninth hour Jesus cried out with a loud voice, saying, 'Eli, Eli, lema sabachthani?' that is, 'My God, my God, why have you forsaken me?'" We might call this the greatest, highest, or ultimate experience of Christ's pure humanity. His entire earthly existence led up to this moment and the fulfillment of the mission that began with his birth.

An Ordinary Early Life

By all accounts the life of Christ was, in some ways, emphatically normal. His family, for example, seems ordinary. The sacrifice of doves or pigeons that Mary and Joseph offered at his birth was the offering designated for people of limited means. (Check out Luke 2:24 and compare it with Lev 12:8 if you want to track that down.) Nazareth was not a special place to grow up and it is still not a special place today, well, if we allow for it now being a tourist magnet thanks to Jesus. It wasn't the capital of anything or a large bustling hub of activity. As a native New Yorker (State, not City), I might think of Nazareth as the Buffalo of ancient Israel. It was certainly much more like Rome, N.Y., than the Rome of the Roman Empire. Nathanael's question, "Can anything good come out of Nazareth?" reveals that people from Nazareth were blessed with low expectations. In this inconspicuous town among unambitious people Jesus spent his childhood and eventually practiced his trade.

He learned his craft from his (step)father Joseph. At a later time, people would question, "Is not this the carpenter's son?" (Matt 13:55) and "Is not this the carpenter?" (Mark 6:3). That tells us they probably worked together, though later, during Christ's ministry, Joseph is absent. He likely died, which then likely thrust Jesus, as the oldest son, into the role of primary breadwinner for the family. As a result, his mother must have counted on him for many things, which would be a disappointment if Jesus ever moved away. And he did move away.

When Christ became publicly active, he moved to Capernaum. This lakeside town with an almost tropical climate must have been a better place to be if you were, say, a fisherman like so many of the disciples, or the Messiah whom the disciples would need to follow. As we now know, some people followed him, and some people did not.

A Life That Becomes Extraordinary

Among those who rejected him early were his own brothers. John 7:5 says, "For not even his brothers believed in him." I am not sure how many useless arguments about religion Jesus got into with his brothers over the years. Maybe not many. He got into those later as people began to challenge just about anything he did or said. My personal guess is that the family in Nazareth was a run-of-the-mill religious household until Jesus began to make it much clearer that he was not a run-of-the-mill brother or son. The separation between him and his brothers became obvious when Jesus left the carpenter's shop to give himself over to the life of an itinerant rabbi. Maybe James, Jude and the rest showed less aptitude for carpentry and now felt stuck. Or maybe they all had other responsibilities and there was no one to take up work in the shop. They may have resented Jesus simply for leaving his tools to begin teaching, working miracles and the like. "Who does he think he is anyway? Too good for us now, is he?" This would all be very typical human stuff. And again, this had always seemed a normal ancient family in a normal ancient village.

The challenges multiplied when he began his public ministry. There were healings and teaching tours and all manner of wonders to be performed. It was tiring work and kept him away from his new home in Capernaum (possibly with Peter) much of the time. Then there were the demons. The Bible is not full of demonic activity as some who rarely read it might imagine, but there surely was a lot of it when Jesus showed up on the scene. I suppose though, it might be taken as a badge of honor when demons oppose you, even if they are not always quite so observable in what they do.

Worse may have been the human opposition that seemed to come mainly from the religious elite. That must have been irritating. All the right rabbis, who studied in the right places and held all the right positions in all the right synagogues – even the priests at the temple in Jerusalem – disapproved of Jesus. You might expect that God the Son, the Messiah and the Sent One, could be given the benefit of the doubt when he spoke up on matters of religion, but no. Somebody always thought they knew better. If Jesus were to turn up today and begin to carry out a public ministry, we can be sure that he would again encounter religious opposition. Much of it would come from scholars at elite universities who are trained to speak on matters of faith. Such specialists often seem strangely out of tune with the Scriptures and spill a good deal of ink explaining what *they do not*, therefore implying what *we should not*, believe. They also tend to focus less on prayer than Jesus did, rarely admitting that they, as we all do, have the vastly greater need. Jesus knew well, and much better than we seem to, his need to rely on his Father. His long and frequent appointments in prayer punctuate the Gospels. Oh, that we would learn such divine dependence! Speaking of prayer, let's stay there for a minute.

Jesus in Prayer

One of the most interesting prayers that Jesus offered was in Bethany at the graveside of Lazarus. After substantial dialogue with his disciples, Martha and Mary, in John 11:41-42, Jesus prays, and here is what he says, "Father, I thank you that you have heard me. I knew that you always hear me, but I said this on account of the people standing around, that they may believe that you sent me." Christ prays out loud for one reason, he says, so that people will know that he was sent by God. He wanted to publicly connect the upcoming miraculous sign to his relationship with the Father, lest people try to connect it with something else. God the Father always heard Jesus' prayers and Jesus knew it. He knew it before he told Lazarus to leave the tomb. But God hearing a prayer is one thing. His answering the prayer in precisely the way we might imagine it is something else altogether. The raising of Lazarus reveals one sort of outcome; Gethsemane provides quite another. Let's look at Matt 26:36-46:

> Then Jesus went with them to a place called Gethsemane, and he said to his disciples, "Sit here, while I go over there and pray." And taking with him Peter and the two sons of Zebedee, he began to be sorrowful and troubled. Then he said to them, "My soul is very sorrowful, even to death; remain here, and watch with me." And going a little farther he fell on his face and prayed, saying, "My Father, if it be possible, let this cup pass from me; never-

theless, not as I will, but as you will." And he came to the disciples and found them sleeping. And he said to Peter, "So, could you not watch with me one hour? Watch and pray that you may not enter into temptation. The spirit indeed is willing, but the flesh is weak." Again, for the second time, he went away and prayed, "My Father, if this cannot pass unless I drink it, your will be done." And again he came and found them sleeping, for their eyes were heavy. So, leaving them again, he went away and prayed for the third time, saying the same words again. Then he came to the disciples and said to them, "Sleep and take your rest later on. See, the hour is at hand, and the Son of Man is betrayed into the hands of sinners. Rise, let us be going; see, my betrayer is at hand."

Jesus was not usually troubled. It is only in Gethsemane that this particular word is applied to him, both here in Matthew and in Mark 14:33. It is no surprise that he prays. He prayed about everything, so how much more should we expect to encounter him praying now in such a difficult time? Luke adds, "And there appeared to him an angel from heaven, strengthening him. And being in agony he prayed more earnestly; and his sweat became like great drops of blood falling down to the ground." When the stress is so great that you are sweating literal blood, it helps to have angels at your disposal. Your human friends are more likely to let you down.

And so they did. It is certainly disappointing, though not a major surprise that the disciples keep falling asleep. How many of us tend to find our minds drifting when prayers get to be long? Christ's question, "So, could you not watch with me one hour?" is more than a little convicting to read. In a time of trouble in the middle of the night, an hour can seem like an eternity. Luke explains that they were "sleeping for sorrow" (Luke 22:45). Any of us might have fallen asleep too. Then we would have looked back and felt stupid that we did not see the importance of the moment when we were in it. A missed opportunity. At any rate, this is not the only time that the disciples of Jesus disappointed him. People will do that, which should teach us to rely upon God.

So, in full dependence upon God, Jesus offers up the prayer, "My Father, if it be possible, let this cup pass from me; nevertheless, not as I will, but as you will." A bit later he says, "My Father, if this cannot pass unless I drink it, your will be done." And after that, he "prayed for the third time, saying the same words again." As we have said in an earlier chapter, not all repetitions amount to "vain repetitions" as the KJV words it in Christ's Sermon on the Mount. Some repetition is desirable. It is an eloquent way to express emphasis that wells up from the heart and has neither the time nor additional energy required for creativity with elaborate words. It is a prayed-out-loud version of *italics,* or **boldface,** or underlining rather than a way to fill up the time. Jesus understood what a big deal it was to go to the cross and these prayers poured forth naturally as a way of getting it all off his chest. The prayer expresses a combination of two desires.

The first desire involves the possibility of not going to the cross at all – of "letting the cup pass" without drinking it dry. Surely, if there is another way, then that other way would seem preferable to dying a distressingly slow, horrendously painful death while bearing the unimaginable weight of the sins of the world. "If there is detour around Golgotha, Father, let's take it."

The second desire is quite as important as the first, maybe more. Jesus wanted to do the Father's will and he always *wanted* to do it. More than that, he *did it without fail*. He was ever the obedient Son. His words and actions were a perfect expression of the Father. Think back on John 8:28-29. "So, Jesus said to them, 'When you have lifted up the Son of Man, then you will know that I am he, and that I do nothing on my own authority, but speak just as the Father taught me. And he who sent me is with me. He has not left me alone, for I always do the things that are pleasing to him.'" This Man who is the perfect expression of the Father, prayed and prayed and prayed again at Gethsemane. God heard him, but he did not answer the way we might have thought best. Then the scene is altered. Jesus speaks the words, "See, the hour is at hand, and the Son of Man is betrayed into the hands of sinners. Rise, let us be going; see, my betrayer is at hand."

Betrayal

Jesus plainly saw through both the character of, and the betrayal by, his disciple Judas. He knew Judas inside and out. Much earlier, in John 6:10 Jesus said, "Did I not choose you, the twelve? And yet one of you is a devil." Jesus knew. There was that strange scene at their Last Passover, when Jesus said to the disciples, "Truly, truly, I say to you, one of you will betray me" (John 13:21). A bit later, as Luke 22:3-4 says, "Then Satan entered into Judas called Iscariot, who was of the number of the twelve. He went away and conferred with the chief priests and officers how he might betray him to them." An already wicked man was now inwardly moved by the devil himself and Jesus would suffer the consequences. Still, God has not lost control.

John Piper once said, "God rules over Satan and gives him no more leash than can accomplish his ultimate goal." [22] The preceding paragraph on Judas illustrates for us Jesus' overseeing of all the events leading up to the cross and his anticipation of the cross itself. There are no surprises here from his standpoint, though there would have been from ours. The disciples did not see this coming, which shows us what our likely level of understanding would have been if we had been there. In other words, our level of comprehension would also have been somewhere around zero. Jesus, for his part, demonstrates perfect control over everything and everyone involved as the whole story is moving toward the cross.

Belittled by his brothers, disappointed by his friends, and utterly betrayed by one of that number. This is no way to treat a Messiah. Looking back upon Christ's life, we said that his father on earth probably died fairly young. Sad, though sometimes it happens. But his Father in heaven was always there for him and Jesus

---

22 John Piper, *Desiring God: Meditations of a Christian Hedonist* (Colorado Springs: Multnomah Books, 2011).

was an obedient Son. Jesus said and did only that which pleased him. Jesus prayed often and the Father always heard his prayers. The prayers in Gethsemane were no different in that regard, but a unique perspective is gained from the book of Hebrews.

Learning Obedience

"In the days of his flesh, Jesus offered up prayers and supplications, with loud cries and tears, to him who was able to save him from death, and he was heard because of his reverence. Although he was a son, he learned obedience through what he suffered. And being made perfect, he became the source of eternal salvation to all who obey him" (Heb 5:7-9). Did you catch that? "He was heard because of his reverence" and yet he suffered. And by his suffering he learned obedience. This is how he became the source of our eternal salvation.

The prayers in the garden were heard. The prayer about doing the Father's will culminated in the cross. Jesus, as always, carried out the will of the Father, not grudgingly, but faithfully and out of love. The prayer that the cup might pass from him, or in other words, that the cross might be avoided, was refused. No matter that his prayers were loud and tearful. No matter that the Father was certainly able to save him from death, in theory at least. This was the reason why Jesus came. There was no way for Jesus to *go* to the cross and *not go* to the cross at the same time. God the Father, with the full knowledge of the Son, made plans for our redemption prior to humanity ever existing. Before we fell in disobedience, heaven preordained that we would be rescued through the obedience of Christ. We needed to be saved from our sins and Jesus was the one sent to save us.

Perhaps, as with the prayer at the tomb of Lazarus, Jesus said these things so that they would be heard and recorded in the Gospels mainly for our sake. Considering how many hours Jesus spent in prayer over his lifetime and how little of it we have written down for us, the notion seems likely. We have exactly and only those words of Christ's prayers that God deemed necessary and intended for our benefit. So, Jesus prayed. As a result, we have moments of insight into the mind and heart of the God-Man as he communes with his

Father. We have a glimpse into the eternal life of the Trinity. And Jesus was obedient. And Jesus learned obedience through the things that he suffered.

Jesus was never *disobedient* to begin with. His relationship with his Father was never that of David with Absalom or Amnon. He was not like the sons of Eli or Samuel engaging in scandalous conduct. Nonetheless, the human experience on earth had something to offer which a purely heavenly knowledge could not provide. Unlike earth, heaven has no sin. Sin cannot survive in the presence of such holiness. In heaven, we will never undergo suffering, distress, or betrayal as we do here, too often and much too severely. Our fathers disappoint, some more than others, and assuming they are present and a part of our lives, we must cope with their imperfections. Just ask my kids. Search as we might, in the eternal interaction of the Triune God, we would never find a hint of disappointment. There is only complete satisfaction and sheer delight. Not being sinful himself, Jesus could not know sin the way we do, from hard, shameful, willful experience. He never sinned against anyone. But he could experience firsthand the effects of sin and he could certainly feel the pain of it just as we do, day after day in our fallen environment. He experienced it fully at the cross.

The cross of Jesus was not the only cross ever constructed to be used as a tool of torture, humiliation, and death. Even on Calvary, two others died alongside the Savior. It is well documented that the cross had been used for centuries before Christ was ever fastened to one with Roman nails. The cross of Jesus was still unique in all of human history because only the cross of Christ could redeem us. This one cross, or more precisely, the Redeemer who died on it, bore the guilt, the shame, and the punishment for our sins. This had never happened before and will never happen again because Jesus was able to cry out "It is finished" (John 19:30).

The Experience of Being Forsaken

His work could be completed only in the experience of being forsaken. The cry on the cross, "My God, my God, why have you forsaken me?" is more than a pointer to Psalm 22. The Father was fully able to deliver him but did not. To do so would have required the abandonment of their agreed-upon plan. Instead of them both abandoning the plan, the Father abandoned the Son and left him to die. The human cry of a son in need of a father had to be ignored and the fact that Jesus saw it coming did not make the cross less painful. It might have actually added to the pain. Being forsaken, ignored, and left to die, gave Jesus the complete and tragic dose of life in a sin-stained world.

The orphan, left fatherless through death or abandonment or both, knows this feeling. It is not a pleasant one. You need help, guidance, or someone to encourage you and tell you to try one more time, and the response is dead silence. If you ask, no one answers, because no one is even there to hear. The child is left alone in a struggle that no child was ever meant to endure. But this is a fallen world, which doesn't work properly. It is not operating fully in agreement with its created intent. Struggle is one attribute of its essence, and no exceptions are made for age, or size or ability – not even for the divine Son of God.

Sometimes the pain or the longing is so great that the child decides, often more by reflex than decision, to pretend that all is well. No pain or longing is there, or so we tell ourselves and (unsuccessfully) try to tell others. That was certainly true in my case. The brain has ways of masking what it really wants to think or feel, allowing that brain's owner to deny the thoughts and feelings as if they were not real at all. If these aches are allowed to see daylight, they appear in strange ways, with floods of hurt and anger that seem to have no cause, no object, and no natural end. If this happens at a later point in life, say in late middle age, there is also conscious embarrassment. How silly to long for a father when you are so far removed from being a child. Here it is helpful to remember the cry of Christ from the cross. A thirty-something Savior was dying and bearing the humiliation that we so deserved. One of the few things he said came in the form of a question directed at the God who was uniquely his Father, which we might paraphrase, "Why aren't you here? Why don't you help me? Why don't you care?" This is the cry, we are told, of one learning obedience.

Jesus was forsaken by his Father. The fully human Redeemer was left on the cross to die in solitary suffering. His precise torment was his alone to bear. No one else had the capacity to bear it and he was required to bear it alone. But it was only temporary. His death gave way to resurrection. His suffering led to salvation. The agony of shouldering the sins of the world was transformed into the means of forgiveness for all who believe. The anguish of being abandoned in a time of such great need gives credibility to the statement, "And behold, I am with you always, to the end of the age" (Matt 28:20).

Trust When Trust Is Difficult

He will always be with us. In both Deuteronomy 31:6 and 8, Moses reassures the people of Israel saying, "He will not leave you or forsake you." In the New Testament, Hebrews 13:5 echoes the same thought, "I will never leave you nor forsake you." We can take God at his word. We need to do so.

The fatherless child, as we have observed, encounters a hurdle when trying to believe that God will always be there. And yet, while fully admitting the challenges can be great, there is a need to encourage us all to move forward. When we don't feel like trusting, we can still behave in a trusting way. We can admit that our lack of trust is unwarranted when we direct it toward an infallibly faithful God. We might confess that our feelings toward God may not accurately reflect his attributes – he who is unchangingly steadfast in his grace toward us. He is with us and that is no small thing. Our doubts tell us much about our own lives and hearts, and about life in a chronically sin-damaged world. The effects of sin are deep and widespread and none of us can escape them altogether. All of us feel them and all of us express them. We see sin's effects every day. This is part of the deep tragedy of sin and why Christ paid such a high price to overcome it. While our doubts reflect well the uncertainty of life on earth, they tell us little about the Life-giver in heaven. Our doubts can project the sin of this world, which we see all too clearly, upon a sinless God who remains invisible to our eyes.

God, who for the present remains unseen, still asks us to trust him. If we do not do so, we only hurt ourselves. He is faithful. He will not forsake us. He will not leave us. If our experience has caused us to be orphaned on earth, God looks down from heaven only that much more committed to our cause. He desires us and he desires that we desire him. His unwavering devotion to us is worthy of our unwavering faith. If we know the feeling of being forsaken by our fathers, let it teach us what Christ felt on the cross. Our suffering can be a little like his.

As we come near the end of these reflections, we have mulled over the topics of suffering and of relating to our Father as a Father and not only as God. Along the way, we have also considered prayer, which is the key way that we commune and communicate with him. The last of these reflections will focus on prayer, namely the exemplary prayer that Christ gave to his disciples.

CHAPTER 13
OUR FATHER

"An almost perfect relationship with his father was the earthly root of all his wisdom. From his own father, he said, he first learned that Fatherhood must be at the core of the universe."
— C.S. Lewis, speaking of George MacDonald,
from his Introduction to G. M.'s *Phantastes*

Prayer is at the core of our relating to God as a Father, which means that Christians need to feel comfortable praying and know how to pray well. We need to take prayer seriously. What better way to dig into prayer than to start with instructions from the Savior? Christ's disciples certainly felt this need. They observed Jesus constantly praying, and they wanted some of that same relationship with God for themselves. Evidently, John the Baptist gave his disciples instructions on prayer but Jesus, up to this point, never had. So, one day they saw Jesus praying and we find them asking him about prayer. "Now Jesus was praying in a certain place, and when he finished, one of his disciples said to him, "Lord, teach us to pray, as John taught his disciples" (Luke 11:1). What follows is one of the two versions in the Gospels of what we often call "The Lord's Prayer." I grew up calling it the "Our Father."

Luke's introduction to Christ's teaching on prayer may be more important than it seems. I have normally focused on the quality or quantity of Jesus' praying but have ignored the profound impression it made upon the disciples – the effect it had on them. By watching and, no doubt, often hearing Jesus pray, they became truly interested in prayer. Many of our prayers may be superficial precisely because we have never, like the disciples, felt the need to be taught by Jesus. We may assume God is satisfied with our prayers if only we are. But that would be getting it backward. In that case, we are looking at prayer as something for us rather than for God.

In the Gospel of Matthew, in the Sermon on the Mount, Jesus gives us his model prayer and begins by contrasting it with prayers that are less exemplary. For someone unaccustomed to relating to a father at all, this is eye-opening. According to Jesus, there are not only best ways to pray, what we might call *best practices* for prayer, compared with ways that are merely less ideal. As Jesus sees it, there are also *incorrect* ways to pray. One example of these has to do with the hypocrites; the other example comes from the pagans. Let's delve into Christ's two bad examples of prayer.

How Not to Pray

The first contrast that he points out is in Matt 6:5-6, "And when you pray, you must not be like the hypocrites. For they love to stand and pray in the synagogues and at the street corners, that they may be seen by others. Truly, I say to you, they have received their reward. But when you pray, go into your room and shut the door and pray to your Father who is in secret. And your Father who sees in secret will reward you."

Christ points out two very different types of prayer. He also makes clear that they do not both have the same value. In response to this, we might divide our prayers into categories based on who is present. We have public prayers, such as those on the street corners, where anyone at all can see. Then there is corporate prayer, where the believing community prays together. This is sort of a middle ground between public prayer and the next kind. Finally, there is private prayer, and this is the kind Jesus says has the highest priority. It makes sense that this would be so if prayer is to be the personal Father-centered thing to us that it was to Jesus. It's not that Christ never prayed along with his disciples. He did and we have the record of it. He even prayed publicly at times, such as at the graveside of Lazarus. Yet, most often, he prayed by going off and getting alone. This way he could be in the Father's presence exclusively. This kind of prayer, between the praying person and the heavenly Father, must be the basis of all prayer.

We are not trying to "be seen by others" like the hypocrites. We want to be seen and have our prayers heard by God. If we are tempted to want to appear spiritual to others, then it is better if no one sees us in prayer besides God. If the reason we do not pray in front of others is because we are embarrassed to do so, then we may still have the problem of desiring to appear spiritual. For example, when praying in a small group of Christians, we may not pray when it would be only proper to take our turn. And we may refrain from praying because we do not believe our prayers will sound as spiritual as they should. This can be evidence of still having a self-centered approach to prayer, when we might rather pray with the careless words and reckless audacity of a child asking for the moon or more from his father.

Again, if God is our Father and we are to relate to him as such, then that one-on-one relationship must come first. Even dynamic corporate prayer, such as that which took place on the night leading up to Pentecost in Acts 2, gets its power from the personal sincerity and intimacy that each believer has with the Father. The experience of God's presence is then made more powerful by these individuals coming together in prayer. As stated previously, however, those prayers we offer in our room with the door shut, where only the Father sees and hears, are the prayers that have the highest value to Jesus. But there is one more type of prayer that Christ criticizes.

In the next verses, Matt 6:7-8, Jesus says, "And when you pray, do not heap up empty phrases as the Gentiles do, for they think that they will be heard for their many words. Do not be like them, for your Father knows what you need before you ask him." A quick take on this problem might seem to make it contradict what Paul says in 1 Thess 5:17, "pray without ceasing." The trick is to keep praying, to pray constantly, without that prayer being full of empty phrases. We have elsewhere seen that the words "empty phrases" are what the Authorized version or the NKJV translate "vain repetitions," or the NASB calls "thoughtless repetition." When we pray, we may be tempted to go through the motions of prayer without getting to the place where prayer is full of meaning. Babbling on and on with long-winded, shallow prayers is no way to pray. Echoing words and phrases meant to sound spiritual but lacking in substance is a poor substitute for actual prayer. Reciting prayers over and over in rote repetition while the mind is allowed to wander is not prayer at all. It would be better to quietly groan before God and admit that we do not know what to say. That would be a prayer from the heart. Still, Jesus gives the disciples and us, words to guide our prayer life.

Praying to Our Father

The whole passage is found in Matt 6:9-13. Let's read it all and then dig into it line by line. Jesus says, pray then like this:

> Our Father in heaven,
> hallowed be your name.
> Your kingdom come,
> your will be done,
> on earth as it is in heaven.
> Give us this day our daily bread,
> and forgive us our debts,
> as we also have forgiven our debtors.
> And lead us not into temptation,
> but deliver us from evil.

Jesus begins the prayer with the words, "Our Father." The most important point of the prayer to my fellow fatherless children may be this one: We have a Father. These are not hollow words of false hope crafted to cover some harsher reality. Not at all. God is not simply like a father. He is the real thing. At their best, earthly fathers begin to be something like him. As we talked about in an earlier chapter, all fatherhood ultimately traces back to the Fatherhood of God. He is the best, a truer and better Father than anyone can hope to have, and he is yours. But he is not your Father alone.

He is "Our Father," meaning we share him in the context of one gigantic family of God. Jesus wanted us to always remember the fact of our fellowship in that great family. Each and every believer in Jesus Christ has been brought into the fellowship that he shares with his Father in heaven. Think of all that time he spent in prayer to his Father on earth, listening to his voice in order to carry out his perfect will. The trust – the implicit intimacy of relationship – it is all ours in Jesus Christ. When we encourage one another in our relationship with God, we are doing so as brothers and sisters in his very large household. This implies a closeness can be present among all of us that we may never have taken seriously, just like the closeness we may have ignored with God. We can learn from one another as to how best to relate to our Father and how best to function in his family. Now for the first request.

The next words are "hallowed be your name." This is the traditional wording, which may or may not be ideal. We do not normally refer to things as "hallowed" in everyday conversation, nor do we usually make a verb out of the word "holy," which is what is happening here. So, the underlying word has to do with making something holy, revering it, consecrating it, or setting it apart as something special. The footnote in the ESV is helpful, "Or *Let your name be kept holy*, or *Let your name be treated with reverence*." In either case, I am reminded of the Third Commandment, "You shall not take the name of the Lord your God in vain" (Exo 20:7). This prayer would be something like the active fulfillment of that. It is asking that God's name be revered rather than belittled.

When we speak of God, we should do so in reverent, respectful terms. We need not put on a holy face or take on a special holy tone of voice to make this happen. That would probably ruin the intended mood. But just as we would expect of a child speaking to or about her father (at least in Bible times, if not in our own), there should be an unspoken honor in any mention of God. An interesting comparison can be made with the "Mourner's Kaddish," the prayer recited Jewish people, usually in Aramaic, at the death of a loved one. It says in part:

> Glorified and sanctified be God's great name throughout the world which He has created according to His will … May His great name be blessed forever and to all eternity. Blessed and praised, glorified and exalted, extolled and honored, adored and lauded be the name of the Holy One, blessed be He, beyond all the blessings and hymns, praises and consolations that are ever spoken in the world; and say, Amen.[23]

Praying like that reminds us how we need to look upon God's name when the prayer is over. "Oh Father, cause your name to be treated with reverence, not least by me."

The next thing we pray is "Your kingdom come," and this reminds us that we should be looking forward to God's kingdom. In ancient times, the Jews often divided history into this age and the age to come. There would come a time when God would finally punish evil, set everything right, and rule through his duly appointed, anointed Messiah. Bible prophecy is loaded with talk of the events that will introduce the kingdom (mostly bad) and then the events of the kingdom age itself (amazingly wonderfully good beyond our imagination). It turns out our Father is looking forward to that day, too. It is part of his plan, and it will be a glorious day when it finally comes. He wants us to pray for it. Another line from the "Mourner's Kaddish" says, "May He establish His kingdom in your lifetime and during your days, and within the life of the entire House of Israel, speedily and soon; and say, Amen." [24]

Since we know that the coming kingdom is associated with

23 My Jewish Learning (n.d.), *Text of the Mourner's Kaddish,* from https://www.myjewishlearning.com/article/text-of-the-mourners-kaddish/
24 ibid

Jesus Christ, the coming King, a prayer for the coming of the kingdom is a prayer for Christ's return. It is, in essence, the same prayer Paul prays at the end of 1 Corinthians, "If anyone has no love for the Lord, let him be accursed. Our Lord, come! [Aramaic *Maranatha!*]" (1 Cor 16:22) We see it again at the end of the Bible in Rev 22:20, "He who testifies to these things says, "Surely I am coming soon." Amen. Come, Lord Jesus!" The Bible's last prayer should be on our lips daily as we pray to our Father that his kingdom would come. May he bring that kingdom age to fruition, speedily and soon, and make it reality in our day.

The early church was focused on Christ's imminent return as evidenced in almost every book the New Testament contains. "Besides this you know the time, that the hour has come for you to wake from sleep. For salvation is nearer to us now than when we first believed" (Rom 13:11). When God's kingdom comes, his will shall be done, but we can pray for that will to be done at the present time. This is a reminder that we owe God our fullest obedience. May we never lose that attitude before our Father God.

The next petition is, "your will be done, on earth as it is in heaven." This is an admission of God's authority and of our implied readiness to submit to him. Just as Jesus always did the will of the Father and wanted to see his Father's will accomplished on earth, we are setting ourselves before God the Father as his obedient children. And there is more, of course. Despite our best and most complete obedience, there are many things we cannot do. We cannot change the course of nations or the direct the heart of kings as God can. We cannot order circumstances or bring about the transformation of someone's desires as we see God doing in the pages of Scripture. In short, we are not God, but he is. We ought to long for the Father's will to be done here on earth, which makes earth a lot more heavenly here and now.

Requests for Basic Human Needs

We now move on to "Give us this day our daily bread." God is our Provider and we must never forget that. To make sure we remember, he asks us to pray for our "daily bread" and the wording is, I believe, essential to the character of the request. It is not a lofty prayer about a house or a car or a career or a wife or a husband. It is so much more basic than any of those. It is the prayer that our Father would provide our plain sustenance, like his manna in the wilderness, sufficient for that day. God wants us to believe upon him for the big things in life, but not only for those. He wants us to understand that we cannot survive a single day without him. This is the appropriate attitude of a little child toward a father. It takes years before a child can begin to understand that she may have a part to play in her own provision. Neither the most deprived child nor the most capable can provide for himself. But then, as we get older our tendency is to be far too self-sufficient. God wants us to grasp that even when we are full-grown adults, throughout our earthly lives, we never cease to need him. When we go out to gather the manna, so to speak, it is he who allows it to fall from heaven into our wilderness. And we must go out in faith to gather it day by day.

Another thing we need daily, like it or not, is forgiveness. Jesus never had to pray this as we do. Sinless in his humanity, he never did anything wrong. He was accused any number of times, but always falsely, and this is where his humanity differs from ours. Alas, apart from Christ in us, we are fallen, pathetic creatures and this affects us in more ways than we know.

And lest unforgiveness be an issue, Jesus words this request for us in a way that teaches us much about ourselves. He says, "forgive us our debts, as we also have forgiven our debtors," because not only do we need daily forgiveness, we also daily need to forgive. We can be hard-hearted individuals, seeking to angrily make the most of the many offenses that come our way. Lawsuits multiply and grudges are held, leading to a bitterness that can corrupt the soul. Asking and offering forgiveness leads the way to peace with God and with others.

I grew up saying this line of the prayer as "forgive us our *trespasses as we forgive those who trespass against us.*" While I do not own a Bible that translates it this way, for trespassing I have good visual memories. Walking distance from my house growing up and surrounded by plenty of other houses was a large swath of wooded land owned by the Reinstein family. Everyone knew that it was off limits to everyone but them. "No Trespassing" signs clearly marked the sacred territory, which I now believe is open to the public and contains clearly marked trails. Nonetheless, easily accessible acres of forest such as this proved to be an irresistible temptation to teen-age boys. I and many others were chased off it many times but have never learned how they so reliably caught us, or at least me, in the act. Such vigilance amidst so much woodland and swamp deserves recognition. Nor do I know whether old Dr. Reinstein and his kin ever forgave us. Anyway, the mental picture of "trespass" and "trespassing" is forever there. We need to be forgiven and we need to be forgiving people. There is a lesson embedded in this "forgive us" request that can help form our expectations.

First, without minimizing sin, notice that Jesus, by instructing us to pray for forgiveness, implies that we will have surely done something wrong. All sin, being against God, puts us in his debt whether or not the sin is directed at anyone else. Second, Christ assumes we will have debtors (call them "trespassers") that we need to forgive. How often are we surprised at our own corruption or appalled at some offense against us by someone else? Jesus is not surprised, and neither is our Father. One of the daily things we should pray for is forgiveness, because it is assumed that we have somehow sinned. Again, we do not want to minimize the debt or the trespass on our part, nor should we overemphasize it. But we do need to admit that it is there and regularly acknowledge it to God. The same goes for that sin against us. We will be wronged – that is the assumption Jesus is making. The world is too messed up for us to go through normal days without someone, somehow, jerking us around, mistreating us, lying, or damaging our stuff. Only a person with a heart ready to let things go can say, "as we also have forgiven our debtors." This is again neither minimizing nor overemphasizing the sin of others. It is saying that we know it is real, but that before God, since we need forgiveness too, we choose not to hold it against them.

Ruth Graham, the daughter of Billy and Ruth Bell Graham, tells a wonderful story of how, after a short and ill-advised marriage, she came home to her parents in North Carolina. As she drove up the long, winding driveway, Billy was waiting for her at the top. When she got out of the car, her father wrapped his arms around her and said, "Welcome home." As she puts it, "There was no shame. There was no blame. There was no condemnation, just unconditional love." The prodigal, a daughter in this case, had come home.[25] Her father was happy when she arrived.

Our final petition is a prayer for our Father's protection. "And lead us not into temptation, but deliver us from evil." As we observed more closely earlier, the world is a cold, cruel place. Worse yet, Satan is looking around seeking ways to destroy us. Let this prayer be a daily reminder that we cannot fend for ourselves. We need the strong, authoritative help of our heavenly Father to save us from harm. Life is full of trials and troubles. May the Father spare us from the testing and difficulties that might cause us to sin or become weary in well doing. Is it okay to pray for relief from our struggles and suffering? Evidently so, because Jesus tells us that this is how we should pray. And then, knowing that our enemy is stronger and smarter than we can hope to be, we pray for deliverance. We do not have to face his terrors on our own. Our Father is ready to protect and to rescue us from danger. When life is too much for us, our Father is more than capable of helping us in our time of need.

These are the things that make for effective prayer. May they help us to relate to God as our Father. Let us learn to approach him as his dear children, with open hearts and open hands, ready to obey but still always ready to receive.

---

25 See "'Welcome Home': Ruth Graham on Her Father's Forgiveness. https://www.youtube.com/watch?v=3J3jb2wiQRk

CHAPTER 14
CONCLUSIONS

I began by saying that I do not find it easy to understand the Fatherhood of God but that I believe many others fall into that same category. Too many of us have had to look at fatherhood more as outside observers than as participants in the life of a family. Looking back on the life of my own natural mother, it seems difficult to picture her home life as one of calm and confident joy in any fatherly relationship. What did she know about her own origins and when did she learn about the circumstances of her birth? We might ask the same question from the perspective of her mother's husband. Did he know the full truth about Frances's conception and when did he learn it? And what sort of complex and problematic emotional baggage did Frances carry into adulthood?

There simply was no substantial legacy of fatherhood that she was capable of handing down to the next generation – only three children with blank spaces on their birth certificates where the father's name was supposed to be. Maybe I would have grasped fatherhood better with either a closer connection or a longer time with my adopted dad. As it stands, however, there is not enough there to look back on that gives me confidence in a developing a father-son relationship with God. Sometimes people ask me, since I did not grow into adulthood with a father, was there perhaps a father figure? My only response is that there were adult men, who might have wanted to help and even did help from time to time, but no, there was no one who took that place in my adolescent vision. And then, this lack of a father to show me the ropes, or whatever fathers do, was certainly exacerbated by having an adopted mother who had her own difficulties. She would have gladly done all for me that was within her ability, but her abilities were tragically limited. Yet none of these deficiencies must be allowed to get the last word.

Sure, growing up I had my issues and some of those have impacted my relationship with God as well as my connections with others. Still, to give in to despair or to succumb to some kind of hopelessness in relating to God would only imply that God is not bigger than my personal problems. This simply cannot be the case.

God has revealed himself thoroughly enough in Scripture to allow us to see that the challenges we face in this world are merely the heartbreaking effects of millennia of fallen human history taking place in a fallen environment. And God is infinitely bigger and better than any disaster that generations of sinful humans or the full army of rebellious demons can concoct to play havoc with his good intentions. He will be victorious in the end. That is why we must approach him with all the confidence that the blood of Christ has bought for us. We need to commit to seeking his face. Our doubts are not bigger than his desire for us. Our troubles, whether self-inflicted or thrown at us from outside, whether accidental or deliberate, are not bigger than his compassion or his care.

The faithfulness of God our Father will see us through to a full realization of what it means to know him. We can expect to grow more and more into his likeness, taking on his character and those of his attributes which we humans can share. There is much to learn about what it means to be a child in his family, especially for those of us that have a limited understanding of family just now. But he knows our need and his compassion will be revealed to us over time. He will not leave us as orphans.

We can trust that the beauty of what is still to be revealed about this relationship will exceed anything we ever hoped or dreamed. The Fatherhood of God should be a caring and calming presence in our lives. We should not let our hearts be troubled. He is the best Father that we could ever imagine – and is still better than that. His Fatherhood so surpasses all human fatherhood that having God as our Father gives us the truest Father of all. The best father on earth cannot compare to our Father God. He is the ultimate Provider and Protector. Even if our earthly mother should forget or abandon us, God our Father is more than sufficient to step in and fill whatever needs we may have. He deserves our complete obedience, and we have an example in Jesus Christ as to what that obedience can look like. It is submission to the will of God in the face of unanswered prayer and compliance when it means death on the cross. Yet, even the most costly obedience will be joyfully worth every tear when we finally join the Father, Son and Spirit in the glory of our eternal home.

Though he is our Father in heaven, we can relate to him intimately in prayer even now. Christ has given us a model which can motivate us in our need to pray and provide an example of what our prayers ought to include. For those of us who lack an understanding of what it means to have a father or never properly learned how to be a father, there is hope. We have the best Father of all. He has spoken to us through the words of Scripture. We never have to feel like we are alone in this world again. He is faithful and we are not orphans. Keep that ever in mind as we bow in worship to him. He is faithful, he is powerful, he is good, and we are his children in Christ.

> Great is Thy faithfulness O God, my Father;
> There is no shadow of turning with Thee.
> Thou changest not, Thy compassions, they fail not;
> As Thou hast been, Thou forever wilt be.
>
> Summer and winter, and springtime and harvest,
> Sun, moon and stars in their courses above,
> Join with all nature in manifold witness,
> To Thy great faithfulness, mercy and love.
>
> Pardon for sin and a peace that endureth,
> Thine own dear presence to cheer and to guide;

Strength for today and bright hope for tomorrow,
Blessings all mine with ten thousand beside!

Great is Thy faithfulness! Great is Thy faithfulness!
Morning by morning new mercies I see;
All I have needed Thy hand hath provided;
Great is Thy faithfulness, Lord, unto me!

— Original poem by Thomas Obadiah Chisholm (1866-1960),
music added by William Runyan (1870 – 1957)

ABOUT THE AUTHOR

A husband, father, and fatherless son, David Kosobucki is the Provost of Horizon University in Indianapolis and pastor of Horizon Central CityWay Church, a church in downtown Indianapolis that he helped start in 1998. Fatherless Reflections is his first attempt at writing for a public audience. Originally from Buffalo, N.Y., he is a graduate of the University at Buffalo and has a Doctor of Ministry degree from Trinity Evangelical Divinity School in Deerfield, Ill.